The Pragmatic
Movement in
American Philosophy

Other books by Charles Morris

Six Theories of Mind (1932)

Foundations of the Theory of Signs (1938)

Paths of Life: Preface to a World Religion (1942)

Signs, Language, and Behavior (1946, 1955)

The Open Self (1948)

Varieties of Human Value (1956)

Signification and Significance: A Study of the
Relations of Signs and Values (1964)

Festival (1966)

THE
PRAGMATIC
MOVEMENT IN
AMERICAN
PHILOSOPHY

Charles Morris

George Braziller

NEW YORK

Preface

This book deals with the main ideas of four American philosophers. Charles Sanders Peirce, William James, John Dewey, and George Herbert Mead. It is based directly upon a study of their writings, from which extensive quotations are made. Its emphasis is upon the ideas themselves and their interrelationships. For this reason the book is not primarily a history of American pragmatic philosophy nor an interpretation of its relation to American culture nor a compendium of scholarly research about this philosophy. All of these matters do enter into the argument, but in a secondary way.

The core stress, to repeat, is upon the thoughts of Peirce, James, Mead, and Dewey. What are the basic ideas of these men? What similarities do they show? What is the source of whatever organization they reveal? This book is a resolute attempt to deal critically with such matters; it asks the reader's cooperation in this enterprise. I like to think of it as a work within American pragmatic philosophy, and not simply a book about it.

All my research assistants in recent years have helped in one way or another to form the content of this book: Dr. Fred R. Berger, Dr. Denis O'Donovan, Daniel Hamilton, B. Wayne Shirbroun, Frank Sciadini, Jan Sugalski, Christopher Storer, Evan Jobe, Dr. Phyllis Meek, Tyson Ritch, Dian Haun. I am grateful to all of them for their contributions. Sydney Beaudet helped on the final typing. Dian Haun prepared the Index. I am also indebted to my colleague Professor George R. Bartlett for critical comments on an earlier draft.

CHARLES MORRIS

Acknowledgments

For permission to quote copyrighted material I am indebted to the following:

The Belknap Press of Harvard University Press, for passages from *The Collected Papers of Charles Sanders Peirce*, edited by Charles Hartshorne, Paul Weiss, Arthur W. Burks, and published from 1931 to 1958.

Roberta L. Dewey, for selections from *Experience and Education* by John Dewey.

Holt, Rinehart & Winston, Inc., for material from John Dewey, *Logic: The Theory of Inquiry*; and John Dewey, *Reconstruction in Philosophy*.

Little, Brown and Company, for material from *The Thought and Character of William James*, by Ralph Barton Perry.

David McKay Company, Inc., for selections from the following works of William James: *Pragmatism*; *The Meaning of Truth*; *A Pluralistic Universe*; and *Some Problems of Philosophy*.

The Macmillan Company, for quotations from *Democracy*

and Education by John Dewey. Copyright in 1916 by The Macmillan Company, and renewed in 1944 by John Dewey.

The Open Court Publishing Company, La Salle, Illinois, for selections from *Experience and Nature* by John Dewey, and *The Philosophy of the Present* by George Herbert Mead.

The Philosophical Library, for a quotation from *Problems of Men* by John Dewey.

G. P. Putnam's Sons, for use of material from the following books by John Dewey: *The Quest for Certainty* (copyright © 1929, and in 1957 by Frederick A. Dewey); *Philosophy and Civilization* (copyright © 1931, and in 1958 by Roberta L. Dewey); *Art as Experience* (copyright © 1934, and in 1962 by Mrs. Roberta L. Dewey).

The University of Chicago Press, and the editors of *Ethics*, for selections from articles by William James (1891) and George Herbert Mead (1930) in the *International Journal of Ethics*.

The University of Chicago Press, for passages from two books by George Herbert Mead, *Mind, Self, and Society* (copyright by The University of Chicago in 1934), and *The Philosophy of the Act* (copyright by The University of Chicago in 1938); and two books by John Dewey, *Essays in Experimental Logic* (copyright by The University of Chicago in 1916) and *Theory of Valuation* (copyright by The University of Chicago in 1939).

Contents

The Pragmatic
Movement in
American Philosophy

I

The Occasion for
American Pragmatism

---

1. *The Occasions for Philosophy*

Wallace Stevens wrote: "The poem is the cry of its occasion." It would not be unfair to express a position found in some American pragmatists in a similar way: "A philosophy is the voice of its occasion"—an inquiry of specific persons directed to the solution of their specific problems under specific personal and social conditions. I do not think that William James would have quarreled with this statement, and John Dewey said much the same (but without the specific stress on the personal factor):

The work of philosophy [is] the old and ever new undertaking of adjusting that body of traditions which constitute the actual mind of man to scientific tendencies and political aspirations which are novel and incompatible with received authorities. Philosophers are parts of history, caught in its movement; creators perhaps in some measure of its future, but also assuredly creatures of its past.[1]

Admittedly, to regard a philosophy as a voice of its occasion is only part of the story. Different persons at different times have somewhat similar problems, and because of this a philosophy—just as a poem or the result of a scientific experiment—can endure and be relevant beyond the occasion of which it is a voice. Further, there are important questions which may be asked about a philosophy which involve no reference to the personal or social conditions under which it arose. But granting these qualifications, it remains true that one illuminating approach to a philosophy is to ask what problems it attempted to solve and for what persons and under what conditions.

A second significant and closely related theme—common, I believe, to all American pragmatists—is the view that every problem (whether philosophical or not) is specific and occurs in a situation many features of which present no problem, and which as unproblematic are taken for granted in attempts to solve the problem. Not everything can be a problem at once; problems can be solved only within a context in which some objects and meanings and beliefs are accepted without question. What is unproblematic in one context may, of course, become problematic in another, but then this new context will in turn contain its area of the unproblematic.

These two related positions are required, I believe, by the pragmatic theory of inquiry, a topic later to be treated in detail. They are brought in here only because of their relevance to the understanding of American pragmatic philosophy itself. If the pragmatists apply these theses in the analysis of other philosophies, it is fair and appropriate that they be applied to their own philosophy.

4

2. *Four Features of the Pragmatists' Unproblematic*

It is believed that there are four main "unproblematic" features in the historic occasion of which pragmatism is the philosophic voice, and that their acceptance by the pragmatists helps to explain whatever unity the pragmatic movement possesses. At the same time, certain of these four features are more prominent in some of the pragmatists than in others, and this fact (linked as it is with the special problems of individual pragmatists) helps to account for such differences as do occur in this movement. In this way both the unity and the diversity within the American pragmatic movement can be made historically intelligible. As of the American nation, so too of its most characteristic philosophy: *e pluribus unum.*

The four main facets of the occasion for the development of pragmatic philosophy were the following: 1) the prestige which science and the scientific method enjoyed in the mid-nineteenth century; 2) the corresponding strength of empiricism in the then current philosophy; 3) the acceptance of biological evolution; 4) the acceptance of the ideals of American democracy.

These four background factors accepted by the pragmatists—scientific method, philosophical empiricism, evolutionary biology, and the democratic ideal—form the "unproblematic" context in which the philosophical problems of American pragmatism appeared and the framework in terms of which proposed solutions to these problems were judged. It is the combination of these

5

four influences, taken together, which gave the distinctive direction to this philosophical development. These four factors influenced all the major pragmatists, but in varying degrees: the influence of scientific method is most evident in Charles Peirce, the impact of philosophic empiricism is strongest in William James, the encounter with evolutionary biology is sharpest in George Mead, the imprint of the ideal phases of American democracy is dominant in John Dewey.

The triumphs of scientific method were, by the nineteenth century, very impressive indeed. The point of view of Newtonian physics seemed only to be strengthened by developments in geology and astronomy. This gave great prestige to the method by which these results were achieved. Charles Peirce (1839–1914), the founder of pragmatism, was trained as a chemist, and spent much of his life as a successful and esteemed working scientist.[2] It is not surprising, then, that Peirce, in his paper "The Fixation of Belief," after considering the major methods by which man's beliefs had been regulated, regarded the method of science as the superior one. Nor is it surprising that he would wish to extend this method into philosophy itself. As we shall see, his formulation of the "pragmatic maxim" was in part his attempt to lay the foundation for a "scientific philosophy." It was on the basis of this maxim that William James developed his own version of pragmatism. A high esteem for scientific method was part of the unproblematic context of every major American pragmatist.

While science was enjoying high prestige at this time, the old belief that philosophy had its own (and even superior) way of knowing was on the decline. That man by "pure reason" alone could delineate the ultimate nature of the universe had been called in question by the work of both David Hume and Immanuel Kant. The result of their analyses strengthened the prestige of empiricism in philosophy: the view that all reasoning about the world should take off from and be in turn checked by "experience"—by what could be "observed." Scientific method itself is empirical in the sense that while it allows great boldness in the construction of theories, these theories must nevertheless be verifiable by experienced data. All the pragmatists were empiricists in this sense. It was, however, William James (1842–1910) who placed the most extreme emphasis upon the category of experience, proposing a method of "radical empiricism" and a conception of reality as "a world of pure experience." This stress comports well with the fact that James was trained as a biologist and became a psychologist, areas in which the theoretical component was less developed than in the physical sciences. It also fits in with his strong sympathy for his philosophical forerunners, the British empiricists David Hume and John Stuart Mill. James's empiricism, however, increasingly took on a more biological orientation than the traditional British version had shown. The impact of Darwin on philosophy was beginning to be felt.

The acceptance of evolutionary biology is the third among the major influences affecting the appearance of American pragmatic philosophy.[3] The major pragmatists all accepted the view that man emerged as one kind of living being within a long evolutionary process. Pragmatism is unmistakably a post-Darwinian philosophy. Its empiricism is a biologically oriented empiricism: "experience" itself progressively comes to be interpreted as

7

involving a living organism and its world. To accept an evolutionary biology raised, however, an important philosophical problem: How is the human mind, human knowledge, human selfhood, human morality, to be interpreted within the evolutionary standpoint? This was a question of central importance for the pragmatists. The most thoroughgoing treatment of the issue was given by George Mead (1863–1931), and it constitutes one of the major achievements of the pragmatic movement.

An understanding of the form which this theory of the human mind and self took on requires the introduction of the fourth contextual factor of the pragmatic movement: American democracy. As members of a young culture trying to build itself in an environment at once bounteous and recalcitrant, the American pioneers felt themselves to be persons who, by taking thought and by acting on their decisions, were creating for themselves a new and more favorable society. They had been, or their ancestors had been, members of European Judeo-Christian traditions whose basic emphasis was upon persons, and their own thoughts of the new society continued this moral tone and ideal cast. Consequently, if biological evolution were to be accepted, such Americans would favor an evolutionary explanation of the human person that would be compatible with human freedom and moral responsibility. Mead's treatment of the human mind and self was of this sort, and eminently compatible with the moral interpretation (as distinguished from a purely political or economic interpretation) which John Dewey (1859–1952) gave of American democracy. When Mead wrote, "In the profoundest sense John Dewey is the philosopher of America,"[4] it is to the moral or ideal aspect of Dewey's interpretation of American democracy to which the characterization applies. For pragmatism is in no sense the expression or justification of all aspects and phases of United States history.

It is all four of the features enumerated, when taken together, that give the distinctive setting and tone of American pragmatism, and which distinguish it from other post-Darwinian philosophies.[5]

3. *Pragmatism, the Practical, and Action*

We shall not at this point be concerned with a definition of the term "pragmatism" but only with some preliminary considerations. Peirce wrote that he was led to the use of the term by reflection upon Kant's *Critique of Pure Reason* (5.3).[6] Kant had employed the term *pragmatisch* to express a "relation to some definite human purpose." Peirce continues:

Now quite the most striking feature of the new theory was its recognition of an inseparable connection between rational cognition and rational purpose; and that consideration it was which determined the preference for the name *pragmatism*. (5.412)

Peirce favored the term "pragmatism" to the term "practicalism" since he held that the "practical" is "a region of thought where no mind of the experimentalist type [such as Peirce's mind] can ever make sure of solid ground under his feet" (5.412). Hence for Peirce pragmatism was not concerned with "the practical," nor even with all types of

9

"practice," but with the way in which knowledge ("rational cognition") is related to human action or conduct ("rational purpose").

This distinction between pragmatism and practicalism which Peirce (following Kant) insisted upon is, of course, not one that common speech makes, as witnessed by the popular tendency (especially prevalent today in political writings) to confuse pragmatism with practicalism. It is interesting that the term "pragmatism" is employed less and less in the later writings of the pragmatists. Even James thought the term unfortunate:

> The name "pragmatism," with its suggestions of action, has been an unfortunate choice, I have to admit. . . . Critics treat our view as offering itself exclusively to engineers, doctors, financiers, and men of action generally, who need some sort of a rough and ready *Weltanschauung*, but have no time or wit to study genuine philosophy. It is usually described as a characteristically American movement, a sort of bobtailed scheme of thought, excellently fitted for the man on the street, who naturally hates theory and wants cash returns immediately.[7]

Certainly for the pragmatists human action is a topic of central concern. This concern, however, is not with "movement" or "activity" as such, nor with all the effects of ideas upon human life, nor with a complete theory of human nature. It is focused primarily (though not exclusively) upon one aspect of human behavior: intelligent action, that is, purposive or goal-seeking behavior as influenced by reflection. Peirce often called this "self-controlled conduct," or conduct "controlled by adequate deliberation" (8.322). He wrote that his theory (which he finally preferred to call "pragmaticism") was based upon a study of that experience of the phenomena of self-control which is common to all grown men and women; and it seems evident that to some extent, at least, it must always be so based. For it is to conceptions of deliberate conduct that pragmaticism would trace the intellectual purport of symbols; and deliberate conduct is self-controlled conduct. (5.442)[8]

Thus it is thinking man, man acting intelligently, that is the center of the pragmatists' attention. This emphasis is clearly compatible with the historical context in which pragmatism developed: scientific method is welcomed by such activity, intelligent activity takes account of observational data, an evolutionary orientation would favor looking at intelligence in relation to problems of acting in an environment, and a rapidly growing America would be sympathetic to a view that saw man as directing his future by the use of his intelligence.

This central concern with man's intelligent purposive behavior throws light upon many other characteristics of the pragmatic movement. It makes understandable why its theory of signs stresses mainly (though not exclusively) the kind of signs which occur in reflective inquiry. It helps to explain why one finds so little explicit consideration of the nonrational, and even antirational, factors in human behavior, which furnish such strong personal and social obstacles to the extension of rational conduct. It even illuminates some of the pragmatists' own valuations, for it tends to set so high a premium upon the "Promethean" or "pioneer" type of person favored by young American culture that it could lead to the neglect and underestimation of other types of persons and value-orientations.[9]

No philosophy, however, can do everything, and we cannot expect a complete theory of human nature from philosophy alone. Intelligent purposive behavior, if not the whole of human behavior, is at least a distinctive and important part of it. Pragmatism is unique among modern philosophies in making such behavior the center of its analysis and construction.

4. *The Sense in which Pragmatism Is a Philosophy*

Man as intelligent actor is in the forefront of the pragmatists' attention. But the human actor, as part of his activity, at times comes to need a comprehensive understanding of himself and the world in which he acts—and in attempting to supply this understanding the pragmatists are philosophers.

To say this implies (at least for purposes of exposition) the choice of a particular conception of philosophy. Some such conception is needed, for even if a philosophy is the voice of its occasion, this does not in itself distinguish it from the many other voices of an occasion.

After the questioning by Hume and Kant that philosophy was in possession of a unique "metaphysical" method to know "reality," the nature and purpose of philosophy has been a topic of lively dispute. There is today no universally accepted answer to this question. Some persons accept the traditional view; some equate philosophy and logic; some regard philosophy as the analysis of science; some think of philosophy as very general moral inquiry; some limit philosophy to general phenomenological description; some see philosophy as the analysis of the meaning of key terms in everyday language; some even hold that the term "philosophy" no longer has any defensible signification.

Even the pragmatists differ somewhat among themselves as to the nature and task of philosophy. But if we look to their products as a whole we find that they have written on logic, on the nature of knowledge, on the interpretation of science, on art, on morality, on religion, on the nature of the cosmos. So for the purpose of this study, in order to embrace such a range of material, we must employ a broad conception of philosophy if we are to regard the pragmatic movement as a philosophy.

We shall follow a tradition that is as old as the Stoics: a fully developed philosophy contains a consideration of methods of inquiry (*methodology*, including *theory of signs*), a doctrine of the nature of value, such as ethical and aesthetical values (*axiology*), and a picture of man and the world (*cosmology*).

In accordance with this conception of philosophy, the chapters to come will be as follows (the first two being a breakup of the topic "methods of inquiry" into two parts): "Pragmatic Semiotic"; "Pragmatic Methodology"; "Pragmatic Axiology"; "Pragmatic Cosmology." A final chapter will contain some generalizations about the pragmatic movement and its relation to American culture. To the work itself is added an Appendix in three parts: "John Dewey as Educator," "Pragmatism and the Behavioral Sciences," and "The Chicago School."

NOTES

1. John Dewey, *Philosophy and Civilization*, pp. 3–4. Complete details as to books and articles cited are given in the Bibliography.
2. Peirce writes of the science of the time as follows:
   > *The Origin of Species* was published toward the end of the year 1859. The preceding years since 1846 had been one of the most productive seasons—or if extended so as to cover the great book we are considering, *the* most productive period of equal length in the entire history of science from its beginnings until now. (6.297)

   Peirce then continues for several pages to list the achievements of this period.

   The material just quoted is in volume 6, paragraph (not page) 297 of the *Collected Papers of Charles Sanders Peirce*. It is customary to refer to the *Collected Papers* of Peirce by a volume number followed by a paragraph number; hence the preceding reference is given as 6.297. This custom will be followed throughout the book.
3. See *Evolution and the Founders of Pragmatism*, by Philip P. Wiener; also *The Influence of Darwin upon Philosophy*, by John Dewey.
4. G. H. Mead, "The Philosophies of Royce, James, and Dewey, in their American Setting," p. 231.
5. It may be remarked that these four "unproblematics" not merely set the context in which American pragmatic philosophy developed, but their interrelations help to account for some of the tensions within that philosophy. Thus some versions of philosophic empiricism (such as "phenomenalism") are at odds with the "naturalism" involved in the acceptance of evolutionary biology. Some interpretations of Darwin challenged the acceptability of democratic ideals. This would also be true of those interpretations of science which stressed rigid and complete determinism. In general there is a tension in the four "unproblematics" between an emphasis upon science and an emphasis upon persons. Hence a philosophy that accepted all four of the beliefs would have to interpret them in a way that made them compatible with each other. The way this was done is an important part of the story of pragmatism.
6. Note 2 explains references to Peirce's *Collected Papers*. Hence (5.3) signifies volume 5, paragraph 3.
7. William James, *The Meaning of Truth*, pp. 176–77.
8. For Peirce's view of self-control, see 5.533–34 and 8.320. He distinguishes a number of stages of self-control. Man has "five or six grades, at least"; the "brutes" are said to have fewer grades.

Peirce's ideas here are of the sort later developed under the concept of "negative feedback." Larry Holmes discusses the details of Peirce's view in his article "Peirce on Self-Control."

9. This is less true of the thought of James and Peirce than it is of Mead and Dewey.

I I

Pragmatic Semiotic

---

1. *The Problem of Identifying Pragmatism*

Pragmatism at its origin did not offer itself as a comprehensive philosophy, but simply as a method of "how to make our ideas clear." Previous philosophies had answers to this question, which is itself part of the problem as to the nature of "meaning," an ancient and perennial problem in the philosophic traditions of East and West. What is historically distinctive of the pragmatic orientation—and as unique as anything in philosophy is unique—is the view that there is an intrinsic connection between meaning and action, such that the nature of meaning can be clarified only by reference to action.[1]

If it is granted that there are no meanings without signs (and this is not always granted), and if the term "semiotic" is accepted as the name for the general study of signs, then the view that there is an intrinsic connection between meaning and action (or behavior) would suggest that semiotic itself be developed as an actional (or behavioral) theory.[2] A behavioral semiotic might then be considered as the foundation of pragmatism, and pragmatism regarded as a philosophy that attempts to deal with the traditional problems of philosophy on this foundation. In this way some precision could be given to the term "pragmatism," namely, pragmatism would be philosophy erected upon the basis of a behavioral semiotic.

The early American pragmatists did not, of course, formulate pragmatism in just this way. Nor did they first work out a behavioral theory of meaning, and then develop their philosophic views upon this basis. Charles Peirce believed that his own philosophic development (and likewise that of James) would not have been basically different if pragmatism had never been heard of (5.466). Certainly he looked upon pragmatism as a support for philosophic ideas which in the main he had developed prior to his formulation of pragmatism.

The situation is further complicated by the fact that Peirce himself had no single clear-cut comprehensive formulation of the nature of "meaning." There is, to be sure, a "hard core" doctrine which is quite definite. But, as we shall see, this is surrounded by supplementations and qualifications which arise out of Peirce's own dissatisfactions with his "hard-core" formulation. It is true that even in these supplementations and qualifications Peirce steadfastly maintained that there is an intrinsic relation of meaning to action—and all who profess to be pragmatists would probably agree with Peirce on this. But a comprehensive and detailed statement of this relation is not easy to give. The issues here are very complex, and no rounded-out behaviorally-oriented semiotic was developed by the pragmatists. To this extent the pragmatic view of the relation of meaning and action, and hence the nature of pragmatism itself, remained somewhat nebulous. An analysis of some of Peirce's statements will illustrate the situation.

A preliminary remark is, however, advisable. So far in these pages we have employed the term "meaning" without hesitation. We will continue to do so, since the pragmatists frequently did likewise. However, as the development of semiotic in recent decades has made clear, the term "meaning" is so vague and ambiguous that it is not wise to use it as a primitive undefined term in the construction of semiotic. In its various employments it covers (at least) intention, signification, and value, as in the sentences: "What does he mean by doing that?" "What does he mean by the word 'equipollent'?" and "Is life without meaning?" Instead of serving as a firm foundation for semiotic, a developed semiotic is necessary to analyze the term "meaning." In this chapter we will at times employ the term "meaning" in an uncritical way, letting the problems this presents arise in the course of the exposition itself.

2. *Peirce's Semiotic*

Charles Peirce is one of the major figures in the history of semiotic. An early article already shows his interest in this topic ("On a New List of Categories," 1867, in 1.545-59). His formulation of the "pragmatic maxim" is a later product of his lifelong work in semiotic.

For Peirce a sign process (semiosis) is a complex process of mediation. Here is one of his more general formulations:

A sign, or *representamen*, is something which stands to somebody for something in some respect or capacity. It addresses somebody, that is, creates in the mind of that person an equivalent sign, or perhaps a more developed sign. That sign which it creates I call the *interpretant* of the first sign. The sign stands for something, its *object*. (2.228)

A *sign*, then, stands (in certain respects) for its *object* by producing in its interpreter an *interpretant*.

Concerning this particular formulation it is to be noted that it does not limit signs to language signs; it does not introduce the term "meaning"; the interpretant is said to be "in the mind"; the term "sign" is not completely clarified since the interpretant of a sign is itself said to be a sign; there is no reference to action or behavior. In general, there is no hint of pragmatism, or the "pragmatic maxim," in this particular formulation.

It is not necessary at this point to consider Peirce's rich, elaborate, and extensive development of semiotic, which is of great significance in itself regardless of its relation to his pragmatism.[3] But something of its complexity may be indicated by pointing out that Peirce distinguished three varieties of representamens (qualisigns, sinsigns, and legisigns), three ways the sign may be related to its object (as icon, index, or symbol), three ways the interpretant may be regarded as related to the object (as rheme, dicent, or argument), three kinds of interpretants (emotional, energetic, and logical), and two kinds of objects (immediate and dynamic).

It may also be noted that Peirce distinguished three branches of semiotic:[4] 1) pure (or speculative) grammar—the general doctrine of meaning; 2) logic proper (or critical logic)—the general doctrine of the applicability of signs to objects; 3) pure rhetoric (or speculative rhetoric, methodeutic, or theory of inquiry)—the laws by which in scientific thought one sign gives birth to another.

Peirce's subdivisions of semiotic are clearly similar to the medieval analysis of semiotic (then called *scientia sermocinalis*) into the fields of grammar, logic, and rhetoric. Peirce was indebted at many points in his semiotic to the scholastics' studies of sign processes. And the general architecture of his earlier semiotic is as innocent of pragmatism as is theirs. In neither case is there any hint of an intrinsic connection of meaning and action.

3. Peirce's "Pragmatic Maxim"

It must never be forgotten that Peirce was trained, and worked, as a physical scientist.[5] In his analysis in an 1878 article ("The Fixation of Belief") of the major ways which have been followed to clarify ideas, Peirce gave the honors to the scientific experimental method. When Peirce considered the task of philosophy and the language which the philosopher should use, he took the experimental scientist, and his use of language, as a model. He expresses the experimentalist's attitude to meaning in this way:

[For] the typical experimentalist, you will find that whatever assertion you may make to him, he will either understand as meaning that if a given prescription for an experiment ever can be and ever is carried out in act, an experience of a given description will result, or else he will see no sense at all in what you say. (5.411)

Peirce, then, in effect, incorporates this position into the "pragmatic maxim." This he states in various ways. Here are three of his formulations. The first is his earliest formulation (1878), though he did not then label it as the pragmatic maxim.

Consider what effects, that might conceivably have practical bearings, we conceive the object of our conception to have. Then, our concept of these effects is the whole of our conception of the object. (5.402)

In order to ascertain the meaning of an intellectual conception one should consider what practical consequences might conceivably result by necessity from the truth of that conception, and the sum of these consequences will constitute the entire meaning of the conception. (5.9; the original is in italics)

If one can define accurately all the conceivable experimental phenomena which the affirmation or denial of a concept could imply, one will have therein a complete definition of the concept, and *there is absolutely nothing more in it*. (5.412)

Peirce gives the following explanations of some of the phrases used in these formulations: "practical consideration" (or "bearing") — "certain lines of conduct will entail certain kinds of inevitable experiences" (5.9); "experimental phenomenon" — "the fact asserted that action of a certain description will have a certain kind of experimental result" (5.427). Hence Peirce was employing the term "experimental" in a very wide way, much as he used "practical consideration." "Intellectual concepts" are characterized as "those upon the structure of which, arguments concerning objective fact may hinge" (5.467).

At the risk of some simplification, these and certain other formulations of the pragmatic maxim seem to involve the following position: *The meaning of an intellectual concept involves an intrinsic connection between action and experience such that if such and such kinds of action were to be performed, then such and such kinds of experiential results would necessarily be obtained.* This we will consider as the "hard core" of the pragmatic maxim.

It is important to note certain features of this position:

1. The pragmatic maxim insists upon an intrinsic connection between action and experience in the phenomenon of meaning with which it deals;

2. The position is not individualistic, that is, is not stated with respect to particular individuals;

3. The stress is upon generality—the reference is to *kinds* of action and *kinds* of experience, and not to single actions or experiences;

4. The various formulations characteristically refer to "concepts" rather than to "signs," so that the relation of the pragmatic maxim to semiotic is not explicit.

Pragmatism for Peirce is essentially the proposal to adopt the pragmatic maxim in philosophy, so that philosophy may gain the progressive and cumulative character of empirical science. If this proposal be accepted, then, he writes:

Any hypothesis may be admissible, in the absence of any special reasons to the contrary, provided it be capable of experimental verification, and only insofar as it is capable of such verification. This is approximately the doctrine of pragmatism. (5.197)

Now the question as to the criterion for admissible hypotheses is the topic of that part of critical logic (or "logic proper") which Peirce called abduction, and critical logic is regarded by him as a subdivision of semiotic. Hence, although the pragmatic maxim is not explicitly formulated by reference to signs, it clearly is for Peirce part of semiotic.[6]

4. *Peirce: The Nature of the Interpretant*

It will be recalled that in Peirce's previously quoted formulation of a sign process, the interpretant of a sign was itself said to be a sign created "in the mind" of a person (a "somebody"). In a late manuscript,[7] not published in his lifetime, Peirce returned to the problem of the nature of the interpretant, and endeavored to remove the circularity involved in defining signs as requiring interpretants which are themselves signs "in the mind" of the interpreter of the sign.

In this paper, after he had established to his satisfaction that the logical interpretant (as distinguished from the emotional and energetic interpretants) "is general in its possibilities of reference, i.e., refers or is related to whatever there may be of a certain description," Peirce draws the conclusion that "habit is the essence of the logical interpretant" (5.486). He does this by ruling out possible alternatives:

Now it is no explanation of the nature of the logical interpretant (which we already know is a concept) to say that it is a concept. This objection applies also to desire and expectation, as explanations of the same interpretant; since neither of these is general otherwise than through connection with a concept. (5.486)

He concludes that habit alone can constitute the generality of the logical interpretant of a sign with "intellectual purport." Hence he can write:

> The most perfect account of a concept that words can convey will consist in a description of the habit which that concept is calculated to produce. But how otherwise can a habit be described than by a description of the kind of action to which it gives rise, with the specification of the conditions and of the motive? (5.491)

And while Peirce holds that "mental facts" are often involved in the production of habits, these habits, he states, "are in themselves entirely unconscious" (5.492).

These points are not new in Peirce's thought. Even in his 1878 discussion of what he later called the pragmatic maxim he said that "what a thing means is simply what habits it involves" (5.400); he had also written that "habit is not an affection of consciousness; it is a general law of action, such that on a certain kind of occasion a man will be more or less apt to act in a certain general way" (2.148)—and even more succinctly, that a habit is "a disposition to respond to a given kind of stimulus in a given kind of way" (5.440).

What is novel, however, is that in the late paper to which reference has been made, Peirce explicitly formulated the logical interpretant of a sign in terms of habit. Elsewhere, as we have seen, he had located the pragmatic maxim within his general semiotic; now he is bringing action (in the form of habits) into the very core of his semiotic. Thus he is now attempting to "prove" in terms of his general semiotic the emphasis in the pragmatic maxim upon action.[8]

Thus there is a strong strain in Peirce's later thought

which, if generalized in a thoroughgoing fashion, would lead to a consistently behavioral semiotic: a sign would always involve a tendency or disposition to behavior in anyone for whom it is a sign.

5. *A Complication in Peirce's Views*

In 1902, after quoting his 1878 formulation of the pragmatic maxim, Peirce continued as follows:

The maxim has approved itself to the writer, after many years of trial, as of great utility in leading us to a relatively high grade of clearness of thought. He would venture to suggest that it should always be put into practice with conscientious thoroughness, but that, when this has been done, and not before, a still higher grade of clearness of thought can be attained by remembering that the only ultimate good which the practical facts to which it directs attention can subserve is to further the development of concrete reasonableness; so that the meaning of the concept does not lie in any individual reactions at all, but in the manner in which those reactions contribute to that development. (5.4)

The general intent of this passage is plain: clarity as to the meaning of an intellectual concept is increased if in addition to applying the pragmatic maxim one ascertains the contribution which the concept makes to "the development of concrete reasonableness." However, considered in detail, the passage bristles with problems, all of which center on the vague and ambiguous term "meaning."

In the first place, the passage brings up the question of the "ultimate good" of the "practical facts" involved in the pragmatic maxim—and one wonders whether the concern has not shifted to the value or significance of signs (or concepts or thoughts) rather than to an expansion of their signification. Thus elsewhere, in discussing the hypothesis of the reality of God, Peirce writes that for a pragmatist the "ultimate test" of the hypothesis "must lie in its value in the self-controlled growth of man's conduct of life" (6.480). Is Peirce not here confusing the signification and the significance of a sign?

Secondly, the explication of "concrete reasonableness" would involve a consideration of Peirce's whole metaphysics and cosmology. So this level of "meaning" seems to rest upon a philosophy rather than in serving as a criterion for the meaning of philosophical terms.

Thirdly, it is not entirely clear whether this enriched "meaning" is over and above the "meaning" delineated in the pragmatic maxim (as the first part of the quoted passage definitely seems to say) or whether certain symbols may contribute to the growth of concrete reasonableness without having "meaning" in the sense of the pragmatic maxim (as might be suggested when near the end of the passage it is said that "the meaning of the concept does not lie in any individual reactions at all"). In any case, the issue becomes relevant when one asks what kind of meaning is had by such mathematical and physical symbols as "incommensurable" and "atom."

Finally, even if "concrete reasonableness" be considered only with respect to "the self-controlled growth of man's conduct of life," it is hard to clarify any particular meaning by attempting to specify this contribution. Certainly all past philosophers would claim that their discourse had meaning in this sense. One might try to deny many such claims by recourse to Peirce's notions of "self-control" and "intellectual concept" (and this might be done with some plausibility), but the issues then become very involved, and those metaphysicians and theologians whose discourse Peirce did attack so vigorously as "gibberish" would not likely be convinced.

The resulting situation seems to be something like this: Peirce did not repudiate his early formulations of the pragmatic maxim, but he did not believe that the analysis of meaning which it embodied (with its stress upon sensible experience following upon action) was the full story—even for symbols with "intellectual purport." The latter is certainly the case, and it is to Peirce's credit that he recognized this. Yet Peirce can hardly be said to have given a clear and cogent formulation of the aspects of "meaning" not expressed in the "hard-core" versions of the pragmatic maxim. In this respect Peirce's semiotic is incomplete.

Peirce does suggest, however, at least with respect to man, that the increment of "meaning" to which he vaguely points is still to be explicated with respect to the context of action. So even here Peirce is holding to the view that there is an intrinsic connection between meaning and action. It is for this reason that Manley Thompson, in *The Pragmatic Philosophy of C. S. Peirce*, was able to maintain that Peirce's philosophy can be regarded as a "pragmatic philosophy."[9]

6. *William James and the Pragmatic Maxim*

It is not uncommon to stress the differences between James and Peirce so strongly that they hardly seem to fall within the same philosophic movement. Ralph Barton Perry wrote: "Perhaps it would be correct, and just to all parties, to say that the philosophical movement known as pragmatism is largely the result of James's misunderstanding of Peirce."[10] Some plausibility is given to this view by the fact that Peirce changed the name of his position from "pragmatism" to "pragmaticism," and this seems in part at least to distinguish his position from James's. He also declared that James's "exegesis" of the pragmatic maxim was "not very deep" (5.13n.). Nevertheless, I think that Perry's term "misunderstanding" is far too extreme, and that while James in certain ways extended the domain of pragmatism beyond Peirce's own views, the two thinkers came out in the end with very similar doctrines as to the nature and limits of meaning. We must now endeavor to substantiate this claim.

The genuine differences between Peirce and James are grounded in the differences of their problems. Stated somewhat grossly, Peirce's guiding problem was to build a "scientific philosophy"; James's "predestined mission," according to R. B. Perry, was "to find a philosophic truth that should justify religion without alienating science."[11] James, like Peirce, was trained in science; he taught science many years before becoming professionally a philosopher. But his training was in medicine and biology, rather than mathematics and physical science, and his own contribution as a scientist was to psychology. In his late twenties he underwent a profound personal crisis, haunted by a deep sense of despair and anxiety. Charles Renouvier's defense of free will came to his aid in this depression, and coming out of this crisis he wrote: "My first act of free will shall be to believe in free will."[12] Religious and metaphysical doctrines served for James primarily as support for the attitude of strenuous endeavor in the pursuit of ideals:

"Other than this practical significance, the words God, free will, design, etc., have none"; "they have for their sole meaning a better promise as to this world's outcome."[13] In general James looked at philosophy in terms of the life-orientation of the individual. He wished to build a "system" of philosophy, to be sure, but while he never turned against science his philosophy never aspired to be a scientific edifice. It is to be expected that James would interpret Peirce's pragmatic maxim in a way compatible with his own conception of philosophy.

In Peirce's 1902 article on pragmatism in James Baldwin's *Dictionary of Philosophy and Psychology* there was inserted a paragraph by James giving the "exegesis" of Peirce's maxim, which Peirce characterized as "not very deep." James there gave the following explication of Peirce's doctrine:

The whole "meaning" of a conception expresses itself in practical consequences, consequences either in the shape of conduct to be recommended, or in that of experiences to be expected, if the conception is true; which consequences would be different if it were untrue, and must be different from the consequences by which the meaning of other conceptions is in turn expressed.[14]

Before discussing this explication of the pragmatic maxim, it will be well to have before us several other formulations of James's views of meaning. In *Pragmatism* he states "the principle of Peirce, the principle of pragmatism" in this way:

To attain perfect clearness in our thoughts of an object, then, we need only consider what conceivable effects of a practical kind the object may involve—what sensations we are to expect from it, and what reactions we must prepare. Our conception of these effects, whether immediate or remote, is then for us the whole of our conception of the object, so far as that conception has positive significance at all.[15]

Finally, a statement from *Some Problems of Philosophy*:

The pragmatic rule is that the meaning of a concept may always be found, if not in some sensible particular which it directly designates, then in some particular difference in the course of human experience which its being true will make.[16]

In terms of these formulations it is evident that there are two major respects in which James's conception of the pragmatic maxim differed from that of Peirce.

First, James's formulations are less demanding than Peirce's early formulations. Peirce had made the connection between action and consequent experience an intrinsic one: only those experiences which were conceived to follow upon the performing of a certain kind of action were relevant to the determination of the meaning of a particular concept (or symbol). The connection between action and experience was thus a relation of "entailment," an "if . . . then . . ." relation of a "necessary" kind. And as we have seen, it is such relations that Peirce intended by the phrase "practical consequences"; James's employment of "practical" is less demanding.

On James's interpretation, instead of an "if . . . then . . ." relation between action and consequent experience, it is an "and" relation, or, even weaker, an "or" relation. Practical consequences are now "sensations we are to expect" *and* "reactions we must prepare"; even less stringently, practical consequences are "conduct to be recom-

mended" *or* "experiences to be expected." The latitude
given by the term "or" in the first (and implicitly in the
third) formulation would permit statements to be meaningful because of their bearing upon conduct even if they
did not predict specific "sensations" or "experiences." That
James took advantage of this latitude is illustrated in the
following statement about religion:

Religion in its most abstract expression may be defined
as the affirmation that all is *not* vanity. The empiricist can
easily sneer at such a formula as being empty through its
universality, and ask you to cash it by its concrete filling—
which you may not be able to do, for nothing can well be
harder. Yet as a practical fact its meaning is so distinct that
when used as a premise in a life, a whole character may be
imparted to the life by it. It, like so many other universal
concepts, is a truth of orientation, serving not to define an
end, but to determine a direction.[17]

The second difference between Peirce's version of the
pragmatic maxim comes out most clearly in the third quotation of James's position. Here the stress is upon *particularity*—that which is expected must be a "sensible particular" and the difference made in a life must be a "particular
difference." Peirce, on the contrary, stressed *kinds* of experience and *kinds* of action, so much so that we have
already quoted him as holding that "the meaning of the
concept does not lie in any individual reactions at all."
James's stress is upon particularity; Peirce's stress is upon
generality. And this difference colors the whole of their
two philosophies.

Peirce is characteristically concerned with the way in
which ideas function in the community of scientists, while

James is characteristically concerned with the ways ideas function in the lives of particular individuals. The "practical considerations" with which Peirce was concerned were primarily the activities of the scientist, while for James they were primarily those activities relevant to the conduct of life of the individual person. The topics of "vital significance" which were central in James's conception of philosophy were (at least officially) outside the province of philosophy as conceived by Peirce.

There should be no minimizing of these differences between Peirce and James, nor their importance for understanding the pragmatic movement as a whole. Nevertheless, on the question of the range of meaning, the difference is in the end not as great as it might at first appear. For Peirce, it will be remembered, admitted a level of meaningfulness beyond that delineated in the pragmatic maxim. Terms and statements were meaningful if they contributed to the self-controlled conduct of life even if they contributed little in the way of specific predictions as to the content of what would be experienced.

Peirce's views on the status of the hypothesis of the reality of God serve as an example. After admitting that only in "exceptional cases" can "experiential consequences" be deduced from the hypothesis (6.489), he calls attention to another peculiarity of the hypothesis, "which consists in its commanding influence over the whole conduct of life of its believers" (6.490). James secured the same result (and as we have seen, expressed it in very similar words) not by speaking of a further level of meaning beyond the pragmatic maxim, but by a looser interpretation of the pragmatic maxim itself.

Thus both Peirce and James pass in their own ways beyond what we called the hard core of the pragmatic maxim. They made, to be sure, different and important uses of this increment of "meaning" in the development of their philosophies, but that is another story. Their total accounts of meaning and its range are substantially the same.

7. *George Mead on Language as Social Behavior*

Mead makes only the most casual reference to Peirce in his writings,[18] and I do not remember ever hearing him mention Peirce's name in his lectures. As an undergraduate at Harvard Mead had contact with James (during the academic year 1887–88), so he must have known something about Peirce, but there is no evidence that Peirce influenced the course of his thought. Nor can Mead be regarded simply as a disciple of James. That he was in general sympathy with the functional tendencies of James's psychology is not in doubt. But whereas James's psychology began and ended with the individual, Mead's characteristic stress was upon the social context in which the individual developed.[19] Thus he became a major figure in the growth of modern social psychology. It is also worth noting that Mead was not a student of Dewey nor was Dewey's thought the starting point of Mead's own development. Indeed, there is no philosopher who stood in the relation to Mead that Mill and the British empiricists stood to James, or Kant to Peirce, or Hegel to Dewey. Mead gave an original and independent accent to the pragmatic movement.

It was against the background of the emerging social

science of the late nineteenth century that Mead's own distinctive orientation appeared. Mead had gone to Germany for his graduate studies, and showed great sympathy for the views on language expressed by Wilhelm Wundt— as two papers by Mead concerned with Wundt make abundantly clear.[20]

In the paper prepared by Dewey for the memorial service held shortly after Mead's death in 1931, Dewey said of Mead:

> In my earliest days of contact with him, as he returned from his studies in Berlin forty years ago, his mind was full of the problem which has always occupied him, the problem of individual mind and consciousness in relation to the world and society.[21]

The problem of the relation of individual mind and consciousness to society was met in Mead's social psychology, while their relation to the world was a central theme of Mead's later cosmology.

Mead gained from Wundt the basic notion of the gesture as an early stage of the activity of one organism which is responded to by a second organism as a sign of the later stage of the first organism's activity. The baring of teeth by one dog is a preparatory stage of its attack, and when responded to by another dog as it would respond to the actual attack, the baring of teeth is a gesture. In a similar way, the beginning of the response of the second dog becomes in turn a sign to the first dog. This reciprocal and continuing process of gesturing Mead called the "conversation of gestures."[22]

Such gestures are, however, nonlinguistic in that the gesture does not have the same signification to the gesturing animal that it has to the animal interpreting the gesture. The true language symbol has, according to Mead, the same signification for the organism which produces the symbol as it has for the organism which interprets it. Mead thought that this development was mainly facilitated by the "vocal gesture"—for the organism producing a sound hears this sound which is also heard by another organism. If this sound became connected in a number of organisms with common dispositions to respond, it could take the same signification to all these organisms regardless of which one produced the sound.

The details and the assessment of this approach to language are not our present concern.[23] Nor are we yet ready to see how Mead dealt with the individual mind, reflective inquiry, and selfhood in terms of language symbols—topics basic to the focus of the pragmatists upon man as an intelligent moral agent. It is sufficient for the moment to stress that Mead's analysis of the gestural sign (whether linguistic or nonlinguistic) made fundamental the behavioral nature of the interpretant toward which Peirce's semiotic had developed. That Mead attained his views independently of Peirce makes the convergence of even greater interest.

The first quotation is from *Mind, Self, and Society*:

Meaning arises and lies within the field of the relation between the gesture of a given human organism and the subsequent behavior of this organism as indicated to another human organism by that gesture. If that gesture does so indicate to another organism the subsequent (or resultant) behavior of the given organism, then it has meaning. . . . Meaning is thus a development of something objectively there as a relation between certain phases of the social act; it is not a psychical addition to that act and is not an "idea" as traditionally conceived. . . . Meaning is given or stated in terms of response. Meaning is implicit—if not always explicit—in the relationship among the various phases of the social act to which it refers, and out of which it develops. And its development takes place in terms of symbolization at the human evolutionary level.[24]

The second quotation, from *The Philosophy of the Present*, shows that Mead explains "ideas" in terms of organized responses, rather than using them to explain the meaning of signs:

One part of the idea as it appears in experience is some perceptual symbol, whether it is of the type of so-called imagery or something seen or heard. The other part of the idea—the logician's and metaphysician's universal—comes back to what I have referred to as attitudes or organized responses selecting characters of things when they can be detached from the situations within which they take place. Particularly do our habitual responses to familiar objects constitute for us the ideas of these objects. . . . The organism responds to these organized attitudes in their relations to objects as it does to other parts of its world. And thus these become objects for the individual.[25]

Mead's most important contributions to semiotic are his behavioral analysis of the language symbol and his elaboration of the key role of such symbols in the development and maintenance of the human self and the higher levels of human society. The importance of these aspects of Mead's thought will concern us later.

8. *John Dewey and the Language of Value*

John Dewey was the pragmatist most concerned with problems of value. He dealt at length with ethics, with social philosophy, with education, with aesthetics, and to a lesser extent with religion. Some of these matters will concern us in detail in a later chapter. What is relevant here is that to a person with such an orientation, the problem of the meaning of value terms and judgments (such terms as "good" and "ought" in some of their usages, and "judgments of value" and "judgments of obligation") becomes of central importance.

Dewey was greatly influenced by Mead's treatment of language—but Mead did not specifically deal with value terms. And while Dewey became increasingly influenced by Peirce (but on these matters after the influence of Mead),[26] Peirce had not explicitly applied the pragmatic maxim to value terms. Whether it can be so applied is an interesting question, but Dewey did not proceed along this way. He wrote of Peirce: "The pragmatic method which he developed applies only to a very narrow and limited universe of discourse."[27] So Dewey went about the analysis of specifically value terms and judgments in his own manner.

Dewey's first analysis occurs in a long three-part paper, "The Logic of Judgments of Practice."[28] A judgment of practice is there identified as a judgment "relating to *agenda*—to things to do or be done, judgments of a situation as demanding action. There are, for example, propositions of the form: M. N. should do thus and so; it is better, wiser, more prudent, right, advisable, opportune, expedient, etc., to act thus and so. And this is the type of judgment I denote practical."[29]

A judgment of practice is made with respect to a situation in which the problem is what to do. As such, Dewey writes, it is "binary":

> It is a judgment that the given is to be treated in a specified way; it is also a judgment that the given admits of such treatment, that it admits of specified objective determination. It is a judgment, at the same stroke, of end—the result to be brought about—and of means.[30]

In this analysis Dewey regards a judgment of value as an instrument for a judgment of practice:

> To say that judgments of value fall within this field is to say two things: one, that the judgment of value is never complete in itself, but always in behalf of determining what is to be done; the other, that judgments of value (as distinct from the direct experience of something as good) imply that value is not anything previously given, but is something to be given by future action. . . .[31]

Dewey goes even further in this early analysis: he suggests that all "judgments of fact" (descriptive and scientific statements) are inseparable from judgments of practice:

> We may frame at least a hypothesis that all judgments of fact have reference to a determination of courses of action to be tried and to the discovery of means for their realization. In the sense already explained all propositions which state discoveries or ascertainments, all categorical propositions, would then be hypothetical. . . . This theory may be called pragmatism. But it is a type of pragmatism quite free from

dependence upon a voluntaristic psychology. It is not complicated by reference to emotional satisfactions or the play of desires.[32]

Dewey's emphasis upon judgments of practice was not always stated in exactly the same terms. In his *Theory of Valuation* he was content to claim that practical judgments may be *grounded upon* factual judgments.[33] And in a late paper "The Field of 'Value' "[34] Dewey went to the opposite emphasis from his "The Logic of Judgments of Practice" and held that practical judgments *as judgments* do not differ at all in kind from factual judgments (that they are characteristically *used* to incite attitudes does not make them different in *content* from other judgments).

Since Peirce did not develop in any detail his analysis with respect to value terms and judgments, and since Dewey did not employ the semiotical framework of Peirce, it is difficult to compare precisely the two men on these issues.[35] The differences do not seem to me to be as great as Dewey's remark on the narrow applicability of Peirce's pragmatic maxim suggests. Dewey's analysis clearly gives specifically value terms and judgments an "intellectual purport" in Peirce's sense of the term—and Peirce would certainly agree on this point (as, indeed, all pragmatists would). I am not at all sure that Peirce's pragmatic maxim cannot cover Dewey's analysis, but if it cannot, then Peirce's inclusion of "contributions to concrete reasonableness" surely can. Peirce even occasionally states the nature of pragmatism in a way almost identical with Dewey's quoted formulation. Thus Peirce writes:

Pragmatism is the principle that every theoretical judgment expressible in a sentence in the indicative mood is a confused form of thought whose only meaning, if it has any, lies in its tendency to enforce a corresponding practical maxim expressible as a conditional sentence having its apodosis in the imperative mood.[36]

It seems fair to conclude that Dewey has made somewhat more explicit certain aspects of the meaning of value terms and judgments which are compatible with Peirce's general semiotic, but which Peirce himself did not specifically develop in detail.[37]

9. *Overview of Pragmatic Semiotic*

The preceding pages by no means cover all that the pragmatic movement has had to say about signs. Indeed, in a certain sense almost everything in this movement is directly or indirectly related to semiotic, since the whole movement is oriented around the topic of meaning. On a number of specific points the discussions in the following chapters will amplify the account so far given. But enough has been said to permit a general overview of the situation.

The most important point is that pragmatism, more than any other philosophy, has embedded semiotic in a theory of action or behavior. The relation of a sign to what it signifies always involves the mediation of an interpretant, and an interpretant is an action or tendency to action of an organism.

Peirce mapped the general province of semiotic and moved in the direction of giving it an actional or behavioral basis—as in his formulation of the pragmatic maxim. This behavioral basis, especially as regards language, was made more explicit in the work of Mead. Peirce himself elaborated in detail only a small part of the semiotic he envisaged. He did not elaborate the theory of indexical and iconic signs to the extent he did the theory of symbols, and even among symbols his focus was almost exclusively upon the kind of symbols which could function in an argument ("intellectual symbols"). He seems to have thought that symbols in art and morality and religion were symbols of this kind, but he never dealt with such symbols sufficiently to substantiate this position. His emphasis was primarily on the designative aspect of symbols, and the relation of this aspect to their appraisive and prescriptive aspects (and to their multiple uses) remains relatively undeveloped.

James in contrast was interested primarily in the meanings of moral and religious terms and the functions they performed in the individual's conduct of life. But he did not expand semiotic in the way that analysis of such terms requires; instead he interpreted Peirce's pragmatic maxim in a manner that accommodated his own interests— and led Peirce to change the title of his position from pragmatism to pragmaticism.

Dewey, with an interest similar to James's, was more explicit in his analysis and believed he had widened Peirce's theory of meaning by an analysis of "judgments of practice" (judgments of what "ought to be done"). While Dewey had a great deal to say that is suggestive about distinctively value terms and judgments, the fact that he did not expound his views within the framework of a general semiotic makes it difficult to compare his views to Peirce's, and thus to answer such questions as to the relations of the interpretants of such terms as "good" and "ought" to each other,[38] and to Peirce's account of the interpretants of symbols.

Though none of the other pragmatists explicitly wrote in terms of Peirce's general semiotic, it is clear that their views of "meaning" may, in retrospect, be regarded as ways of filling in some areas of the semiotic field which Peirce had mapped out. This expanded semiotic, while not labeled as such, and while not systematically organized, contains much material on the designative, appraisive, and prescriptive aspects of signification, and on some of the uses and functions of signs in individual and social behavior. It is by no means a "complete" semiotic: many types of discourse are neglected and the malfunctioning of signs in the individual and society is largely ignored. But though fragmentary, the semiotic of the pragmatic movement helped lay the foundations for the vastly extended range of inquiry which characterizes present activities in this field. Like most features of the pragmatic movement, its behaviorally oriented semiotic opened a door upon a much wider domain than it itself fully explored.[39]

NOTES

1. C. I. Lewis, in a paper on Dewey's logic entitled "Meaning and Action," recognized the doctrine of an intrinsic connection between meaning and action as the distinctive feature of Dewey's *Logic*. H. S. Thayer utilizes Lewis's phrase as the title of his recent book, *Meaning and Action: A Critical History of Pragmatism*. Thayer's book is a major attempt to chronicle and assess pragmatic philosophy as a whole, in its European as well as its American phases. I regard it as the most valuable single book to supplement the present work. Since this work was largely written before Thayer's book appeared in 1968, I was not able to make as much use of Thayer's book as it warrants.

2. There are problems in the relations of the terms "action," "behavior," and "conduct." Currently the term "behavior" is widely employed (as in the phrase "the behavioral sciences"), but a growing number of psychologists object to its application to man. The early pragmatists more often used the terms "action" or "conduct." Where a distinction is not important, "behavior" and "action" will be here employed interchangeably. But it must be carefully noted that use of the term "behavior" does not involve a commitment to the "behaviorism" of John B. Watson. None of the pragmatist philosophers have been "behaviorists" in this restricted sense. The behavioral (or actional) emphasis long antedated Watsonian behaviorism; indeed, it has more in common with Aristotle than with Watson. Dewey's famous paper on "The Reflex Arc Concept in Psychology," published in 1896, while pre-Watsonian, is in effect a criticism of what Watsonian behaviorism came to stand for. And Mead in *Mind, Self, and Society* explicitly contrasted his behavioral approach to Watson's. As a student of Mead I came to employ the term "behavior" in his sense, and to use it freely. If the present-day reader is bothered by the terms "behavior" and "behavioral" he can in what follows substitute the terms "action" and "actional." The sense in which the pragmatists' conception of action involves orientation to a "goal" will become clearer as the argument develops.

3. Peirce's semiotic is found throughout the volumes of his *Collected Papers*, but a substantial part of it is in volume 2 (to be supplemented by the material in volume 8 from Peirce's correspondence with Lady Welby). In spite of the great amount of work done on Peirce, there does not yet exist a comprehensive study of his semiotic. A good preliminary to this, but restricted in scope as its title suggests, is *Peirce's Theory of Signs as Foundation for Pragmatism*, by John J. Fitzgerald. There is a Ph.D. dissertation by Tora Kay Lanto Bikson, "Peirce's Logic Treated as Semiotic," but this extensive work has little to say about Peirce's pragmatism. Among the historically useful articles are: William P. Alston, "Pragmatism and the Theory of Signs in Peirce"; Ernest Nagel, "Charles Peirce's Guess at the Riddle"; and Arthur W. Burks, "Icon, Index, and Symbol." There are a number of articles in *The Transactions of the Charles S. Peirce Society* on phases of Peirce's semiotic (such as those by Thomas A. Goudge, Richard M. Martin, J. Jay Zeman, and Gary Sanders).

4. See 2.229; also 1.559.

5. See the papers by the physicist Victor F. Lenzen: "Charles S. Peirce as Astronomer," and "The Contributions of Charles S. Peirce to Methodology." Professor Lenzen has other such studies in preparation.

6. For pragmatism as the logic of abduction see 5.180–212; also the writings of Alston and Fitzgerald cited in note 3 of the present chapter.

7. 5.464–96. The material is there entitled "A Survey of Prag-
    maticism," and dated by the editors as "c. 1906."
8. Fitzgerald, in *Peirce's Theory of Signs as Foundation for Prag-
    matism*, is especially concerned with the nature of the "proof"
    of the pragmatic maxim within Peirce's semiotic. Fitzgerald does
    not quite claim that the maxim can be formally deduced from
    semiotical principles, but he wishes to go as far as possible in
    this direction. Peirce in 1905 wrote: "This maxim is put forth
    . . . as a far-reaching theorem solidly grounded upon an elaborate
    study of the nature of signs" (8.191). Peirce does often speak of
    his "proofs" of the pragmatic maxim, but I do not believe that
    he claims any such proof is a purely formal deduction from
    semiotical principles. Peirce early held that philosophy should
    trust "rather to the multitude and variety of its arguments than
    to the conclusiveness of any one" (5.265). Peirce certainly con-
    ceived of the pragmatic maxim as an integral and well-grounded
    part of his semiotic. Fitzgerald's book does well to stress this.
9. The question still remains important for Peirce scholars whether
    Peirce did or did not differ in his earlier and later conceptions
    of the pragmatic maxim, and hence in his conception of prag-
    matism. Dewey had argued in "The Pragmatism of Peirce" that
    there was at the most a change of emphasis; Murray Murphey
    and John Fitzgerald find no important differences; Peirce too
    seemed to think he had not changed. In a statement written
    "c. 1910" (according to his editors), Peirce gives the impression
    that he is stating the same doctrine which he "formulated in
    1873," but his formulation is now as follows:

    > [For pragmatism] the true meaning of any product of the
    > intellect lies in whatever unitary determination it would
    > import to practical conduct under any and every conceivable
    > circumstance, supposing such conduct to be guided by re-
    > flexion carried to an ultimate limit. (6.490)

    This formulation seems to differ considerably from earlier formu-
    lations in that it makes no explicit reference to experiential
    effects following upon a kind of action. Might, however, the
    phrase "practical conduct" in the quotation at least implicitly
    involve such reference?
    It is true that around 1904 (as dated by the editors) Peirce
    still wrote that "the *whole* of the purport of the word, the *entire*
    concept" is given by "the conceivable practical consequences"
    (8.191). But note that Peirce now defines "practical conse-
    quences" as "the consequences for deliberate self-controlled con-
    duct"—which seems to differ considerably from the statement in
    5.9 that "practical considerations" means that "certain lines of
    conduct will entail certain kinds of inevitable experiences."
    Peirce himself writes of his formulation given in 8.191 that
    "the sedulous exclusion from this statement of reference to sen-
    sation is specially to be remarked." Thus in the 8.191 formula-
    tion the place of experience in meaning has either dropped out
    or at least become nebulous.

I think that the apparent differences between Peirce's earlier and later formulations of the pragmatic maxim (and hence of pragmatism) warrant more discussion. The difficulties at this point seem to me to show a confusion in Peirce between the signification and significance (or value) of signs. But even if this is so, the confusion is in a way to Peirce's credit, for it shows his sensitivity to the need for a more complete semiotic than he was able at first to formulate: the reference of signs to observable phenomena is not their whole story. Yet it remains part of their story, and certainly Peirce never wishes to deny this. In my reading of him, Peirce remains an empiricist, though not a naive and simple one.

A reader interested in these problems might do well to consult Manley Thompson's *The Pragmatic Philosophy of C. S. Peirce* for a detailed analysis of the notion of concrete reasonableness in relation to Peirce's views on meaning, especially in connection with the concept of God. And also to consult Dewey's article, "The Pragmatism of Peirce"; Murray G. Murphey, *The Development of Peirce's Philosophy*, pp. 361–66; and the book by Justus Buchler, *Charles Peirce's Empiricism*.

10. Ralph Barton Perry, *The Thought and Character of William James*, vol. 2, p. 409.
11. *Ibid.*, vol. 2, p. 230.
12. *Ibid.*, vol. 1, pp. 121, 127.
13. *Ibid.*, p. 323.
14. Peirce's 1902 article on pragmatism, including the paragraph by James, is reprinted in Peirce, *Collected Papers*, 5.2.
15. William James, *Pragmatism*, pp. 46–47.
16. William James, *Some Problems of Philosophy*, p. 60.
17. Quoted in R. B. Perry, *op. cit.*, vol. 1, p. 503.
18. In his late paper, "The Philosophies of Royce, James, and Dewey, in their American Setting," Mead refers several times to "Peirce's laboratory habit of mind," but without elaboration.
19. Mead's son, Dr. Henry C. A. Mead, writes of Mead's early reading in "Macauley, Buckley, and Motley," who "opened the door to him for the magnificent drama of conflicting social forces" (p. lxxxv of Mead's *The Philosophy of the Act*).
20. G. H. Mead, "The Relations of Psychology and Philology" and "The Imagination in Wundt's Treatment of Myth and Religion."
21. Dewey's address, "George Herbert Mead," appeared in the 1931 *Journal of Philosophy*.
22. Wundt had referred to "the backward and forward interchange of gestures." Mead quotes this in "The Relations of Psychology and Philology," p. 881.
23. Mead's preferred term was "significant symbol" for what we have here called "language symbol." Language is discussed throughout his works. *Mind, Self, and Society* is a main source. "A Behavioristic Account of the Significant Symbol" gives a condensed version of his views. For critical discussions see my *Signs, Language, and Behavior*, chapter II, and "A Behavioristic

45

THE PRAGMATIC MOVEMENT IN AMERICAN PHILOSOPHY

Account of the Logical Function of Universals," by John M. Brewster.

24. *Mind, Self, and Society*, pp. 75–76.

25. *The Philosophy of the Present*, pp. 75–76.

26. In my *Six Theories of Mind*, p. 322, there is the following quotation taken from a letter by Dewey: "I should be glad to have the statement of my indebtedness to Mead made even stronger. It stems in part from Peirce and Royce, but only after and through Mead." Chapter 5 ("Nature and Communication") of Dewey's *Experience and Nature*, has many points in common with Mead's treatment of language.

27. From Dewey's article "The Development of American Pragmatism," originally published in French in 1922.

28. This essay originally appeared in three parts in the *Journal of Philosophy*, 12, 1915, pp. 505–23, 533–43. It was reprinted with some changes in the 1916 *Essays in Experimental Logic*; the references in the text are to this work.

29. *Essays in Experimental Logic*, p. 335.

30. *Ibid.*, p. 340.

31. *Ibid.*, p. 361.

32. *Ibid.*, p. 347. The term "reference" in this passage is somewhat misleading; it might suggest that judgments of fact simply *are* judgments of practice.

33. *Theory of Valuation*, pp. 22–24, 51–52.

34. In *Value: A Cooperative Inquiry*, edited by Ray Lepley, pp. 64–77.

35. Peirce recognized three kinds of interpretants of symbols: the emotional, the energetic, and the logical (5.475–76; 8.314–15). Could these be regarded as possible bases for the differences of meaning of judgments of value, of obligation, and of fact? Peirce's treatment of the emotional and energetic interpretants is so fragmentary that to claim such a relation would be hazardous; perhaps these interpretants are more closely related to Peirce's categories of Firstness and Secondness than to appraisive and prescriptive signification.

36. 5.18.

37. A fuller account of Dewey's position on these matters would have to take account of his treatment of the meaning of works of art. *Art as Experience* contains his distinction between "sense" and "signification"; it is in terms of "sense" that he ascribes "expressive meaning" to a work of art. A possible semiotical interpretation of this concept is suggested in chapter IV, section 8, of the present work.

38. C. I. Lewis made a much sharper distinction between "good" and "ought," and hence between judgments of value and judgments of obligation, than did Dewey. The former is dealt with at length in *An Analysis of Knowledge and Valuation*; the latter is approached in a preliminary way in *The Ground and Nature of the Right*. In these books, and in *Mind and the World Order*,

Lewis made important contributions to all aspects of pragmatic semiotic.

39. My own work in *Signs, Language, and Behavior*, supplemented by the later study *Signification and Significance*, might be regarded as a way to organize and to extend the contributions to semiotic by the various pragmatist philosophers. It was not done, however, with any such goal explicitly in mind. My own work started from Mead and not from Peirce; the influence of Dewey, Lewis, Peirce (and Rudolf Carnap), came later, and in that order.

47

I I I

Pragmatic Methodology

1. *General Orientation*

The term "methodology"—not much used by the pragmatists themselves—is employed here to cover the problem area traditionally called epistemology (the theory of knowledge). But since many traditional and current conceptions of epistemology are rejected by the pragmatists, it would be misleading to use the term epistemology in the title of this chapter. The most appropriate title might be "pragmatic theory of inquiry," but the reasons for this would only become clear as the analysis advances.

The pragmatists frequently employ the term "epistemology" in a disparaging sense, as referring to something they have in fact avoided. This is because for Descartes, and much of post-Cartesian philosophy, epistemology was conceived as the problem of how a person can infer from an intuitive knowledge of his own "private mental states" the existence of other minds and nonmental objects. The problem was sometimes stated in terms of "experience": how can one transcend in knowledge his own experience, where experience is conceived as "mental" and "subjective"?

The pragmatists regarded this as a pseudoproblem, resting upon false conceptions of experience, knowledge, and mind. Insofar as "epistemology" had become identified with this problem, the pragmatists shied away from the use of the term. Their own "theory of knowledge" is developed in terms of a different conception of experience and mind.

The pragmatic movement was from the start essentially anti-Cartesian and "anti" those aspects of British empiricism which it shared with Cartesianism. Peirce in 1868, in three long articles in the *Journal of Speculative Philosophy*, attempted to formulate "the spirit of Cartesianism," and to deny by an extended argument the main principles upon which it rested.[1] He stated his conclusions as follows (5.265):

1. We have no power of Introspection, but all knowledge of the internal world is derived by hypothetical reasoning from our knowledge of external facts.
2. We have no power of Intuition, but every cognition is determined logically by previous cognitions.
3. We have no power of thinking without signs.
4. We have no conception of the absolutely incognizable.

Hence for Peirce knowing was not conceived as a process resting upon intuitive knowledge of ourselves which we then somehow attempted to extend to other things outside of ourselves which we do not intuit. But if knowing, and its product, knowledge, is not to be approached within the Cartesian framework, where and how are they to be studied? The major answer in the pragmatic movement becomes: in the study of inquiry, i.e., by inquiry into inquiry.

2. *Peirce's Conception of Inquiry*

Peirce's original conception of inquiry was given in an 1877 article, "The Fixation of Belief."[2] The position taken, as Max H. Fisch has shown,[3] was very close to that of the English psychologist Alexander Bain. Peirce himself in his later thought qualified his early position to such an extent that some of his commentators attribute to him a second theory of inquiry.[4] But the original formulation was of such historical importance in the development of pragmatism that it must here be taken as basic. It is often called "the doubt/belief theory of inquiry." In the 1877 article the term "inquiry" is used to denote the struggle to pass from "the irritation of doubt" to a "state of belief"— though Peirce admitted even then "that this is sometimes not a very apt designation" (5.374). He continues:

> The irritation of doubt is the only immediate motive for the struggle to attain belief. . . . With the doubt, therefore, the struggle begins, and with the cessation of doubt it ends. Hence, the sole object of inquiry is the settlement of opinion. (5.375)

Peirce then considers four methods for the fixation of belief. In the method of tenacity one simply attempts to remove doubt by a vigorous endeavor to reaffirm, and thus hold on to, the belief which one has begun to doubt. In the method of authority one seeks to remove doubt by submitting one's beliefs to those of an accepted authority. In the *a priori* method one accepts after argument those beliefs which one finds most congenial—one thinks "as one is inclined to think" (5.385). Peirce states that most philosophers have followed the *a priori* method; Descartes is specifically given as an example (5.391). The fourth method, which Peirce himself accepted, and advocated for philosophy, is the method of science.

The article "The Fixation of Belief" does not attempt to characterize the scientific method in much detail—this is done in other articles and indeed in Peirce's work as a whole. But a general feature of scientific method is there given in the following terms. It is a method

by which our beliefs may be determined by nothing human, but by some external permanency—by something upon which our thinking has no effect. . . . It must be something which affects, or might affect, every man. And, though these affections are necessarily as various as are individual conditions, yet the method must be such that the ultimate conclusions of every man shall be the same. Such is the method of science. (5.384)

Scientific method, so conceived, is a method which if continually followed would ultimately lead every scientific inquirer to the same conclusion.

The relation of belief to habit is developed in the companion article "How to Make Our Ideas Clear," which appeared a year later in the same journal.[5] Here we have, as already noted in the preceding chapter, the first formulation of the pragmatic maxim, though that label is not yet used. The emphasis which Bain laid on the relation of belief to habit is now strongly emphasized:

The whole function of thought is to produce habits of action . . . what a thing means is simply what habit it involves . . . there is no distinction of meaning so fine as to consist in anything but a possible difference of practice. (5.400)

We have noted in the previous chapter Peirce's reaction to this early formulation of meaning, and his extension of "meaning" to embrace the contribution of a term to the attainment of the goal of concrete reasonableness. It is now to be noted that his theory of inquiry was correspondingly altered.[6] Inquiry is later said to be motivated by "an attraction for the idea itself" (6.307), and ideas are presumably attractive according to their potential contribution to the intrinsic and final attractiveness attributed to the goal of concrete reasonableness. The original stress upon inquiry as the resolution of doubt into belief gives way to the placing of inquiry within Peirce's idealistic metaphysics. It was, of course, Peirce's earlier view of inquiry, and not the later complications of his thought, which was influential upon the historical development of the pragmatic theory of inquiry.

3. Dewey's Views on Inquiry

Dewey's *Logic: The Theory of Inquiry*, published in 1938, is the most mature formulation of his methodological position, but it is the continuation of the direction indicated in his earlier works, *Essays in Experimental Logic* and *How We Think*. There is evidence that Peirce's "The Fixation of Belief" influenced Dewey early in his career, and even in the *Logic*, where he is concerned to maintain the similarity of his views on "logic" to those of Peirce, one of his main references to Peirce is to material in "The Fixation of Belief" paper.[7] An attempt will be made to show that the work of Dewey and Peirce in this area is indeed complementary, even though Peirce reacted violently against Dewey's early formulation of his (Dewey's) position. There are, nevertheless, certain characteristic and important differences in emphasis that should first be noted.

One of these is Dewey's stress in the *Logic* upon the *problematic* character of a *situation* as initiating inquiry, rather than upon the psychological state of doubt. In the early pages of his *Logic* he writes of inquiry as the resolution of an "indeterminate situation" into a "determinate situation." But in the development of his argument it becomes evident that "indeterminate" can be rendered by "problematic," and that the problematic character of the situation involves the interruption or disturbance of ongoing action.[8] Though the stress is thus somewhat different from Peirce's early formulation, doubt would seem to involve the unsettling of a habitual mode of action.

A second difference comes from the stress upon "situation." If the disturbance of action is in a specific situation, then the solution of an inquiry would presumably be found in the continuance of action in that specific situation. One might try to argue that Peirce should hold the same position, since a specific doubt must have a specific locus and a specific resolution. Nevertheless, Peirce does not in fact stress specific inquirers in specific situations. His emphasis is rather upon a community of inquirers, and the "habit" which inquiry is to form is stated in terms of "how it might lead us to act, not merely under such circumstances as are likely to arise, but under such as might possibly occur, no matter how improbable they may be" (5.400). The difference this emphasis makes will show itself in later discussions of truth and knowledge. Dewey, in a distinction he makes between "judgment" and "proposition" can, at least to some degree, find a place in his own account for Peirce's emphasis. Nevertheless, the stress on the specificity of the situations calling out and terminating inquiry, which is found in Dewey (and in James and Mead), is one of the salient contrasts between Peirce and the other major pragmatists.

Thirdly, and even more important, is Dewey's position that the "judgment" is the actual conversion of a problematic ("indeterminate") situation into an unproblematic ("determinate") situation. (The terminal "proposition," in contrast to the judgment, is merely the symbolic expression of the judgment, and so remains available for use in other situations.) [9] There is something almost paradoxical here: for Peirce, an experimental scientist, inquiry terminates in a change of *belief*; for Dewey, not an experimental scientist, inquiry terminates in a change in the *situation*. It is as if Dewey is more "experimental" than Peirce. Now Peirce himself, in the pragmatic maxim, insisted that meaning involved action, but such action was necessary to get the sensible evidence to warrant the formation of a new belief; while this involves in a way a change in the immediate situation, the change is not—as it is for Dewey— the transformation of the situation itself from problematic to unproblematic.

The three differences that have been listed are genuine and important. They seem to be related to the fact that Dewey's basic orientation was to moral inquiry while

Peirce's was to inquiry as carried on by the natural scientist. After some consideration of the relation of logic to inquiry, we will return to the claim that in spite of these differences in emphasis, the general views of Peirce and Dewey with respect to inquiry are basically the same.

4. *Logic and Inquiry*

The title of Dewey's major book in this area (*Logic: The Theory of Inquiry*) identifies logic with the theory of inquiry. Dewey clearly thought that in this respect he was working in the tradition of Peirce:

As far as I am aware, he was the first writer on logic to make inquiry and its methods the primary and ultimate source of logical subject matter. (*Logic*, p. 9n.)

Dewey regards his own account of logical principles (which we will shortly consider) as "a free rendering of Peirce" (*Logic*, p.14, *n.*4). How then explain Peirce's 1905 letter to Dewey[10] in which he stated that Dewey's view "certainly forbids all such researches as those which I have been absorbed in for the last eighteen years"?

The difference is in part terminological. Peirce employed the term "logic" more widely than usual. In its "general sense" he regarded it as "only another name for *semiotic* . . . , the quasi-necessary, or formal, doctrine of signs" (2.227).[11] Within logic in this general sense he recognized (as has been noted) three subdivisions. One of these, "critical logic" or "logic proper," was the theory of inferences (abductive, deductive, and inductive). But

Peirce also had a subdivision of semiotic (and so of "logic" in the general sense) which he called by various names: "speculative rhetoric," "methodeutic," and even "theory of inquiry" (2.106). He speaks of this third subdivision of semiotic as "the highest and most living branch of logic."

Hence Dewey's conception of "logic" as the theory of inquiry might be regarded as developing this third subdivision of "logic" in Peirce's general sense of the term, while Peirce's own work, which he felt was threatened by Dewey, was primarily in the field of critical logic. Thus the apparent difference is primarily terminological. Since most contemporary logicians do not use "logic" in the sense of the theory of inquiry, some persons sympathetic to Dewey's book (such as C. I. Lewis) regretted Dewey's employment of the term "logic" in its title. Dewey himself, I believe, admitted that perhaps the book might have better been called simply *The Theory of Inquiry*.[12]

There is, however, a point worth mentioning that is not terminological but historical. Peirce's main work as logician was on "critical logic," and concerned primarily with detailed analyses of modes of inference. Dewey's early writings on "logic" did not develop or stress the "formal" aspect of logic. Thus Peirce's fear that Dewey's view had no place for his own dominant and characteristic emphasis in logic. This is certainly not true, however, of Dewey's developed position as presented in *Logic: The Theory of Inquiry*.

For Peirce there are three modes of inference: abduction (or hypothesis), deduction, and induction. Inference in each mode requires in addition to premises a "leading principle":

a leading principle is a habit or method which always leads to truth *or* leads to an indefinite approximation to the truth *or* is generally conducive to the ascertainment of truth. (2.354)

Leading principles are "formal" or "material"—the first kind being true in every instance it governs. Thus the formal leading principle for the syllogism in *Barbara* (all *a* is *b*, all *b* is *c*, therefore, all *a* is *c*) is interpreted by Peirce as a general principle of semiotic:

If one sign denotes generally everything denoted by a second, and this second denotes generally everything denoted by a third, then the first denotes generally everything denoted by the third. (5.320)

What is the status of such formal (or "logical") principles in Dewey's analysis? He states his general position as follows:

All logical forms (with their characteristic properties) arise within the operation of inquiry and are concerned with control of inquiry so that it may yield warranted assertions. This conception implies much more than that logical forms are disclosed or come to light when we reflect upon processes of inquiry that are in use. Of course it means that; but it also means that the forms *originate* in operations of inquiry. (*Logic*, pp. 3–4)

And with specific reference to logical *principles*:

These guiding logical principles are not *premises* of inference or argument. . . . They are formulations of ways of treating subject-matter that have been found to be so determinative of sound conclusions in the past that they are taken

57

THE PRAGMATIC MOVEMENT IN AMERICAN PHILOSOPHY

to regulate further inquiry until definite grounds are found for questioning them. (*Logic*, p. 13)

Thus for Dewey logical principles are "*operationally a priori* with respect to further inquiry"; "they are both postulates *and* stipulations."[13] In this way Dewey finds a place for formal logical principles in his general theory of inquiry. In a similar way he is able to account for and to justify the analytic nonexistential propositions of mathematics. Mathematical discourse, he writes,

is itself formed on the ground of freedom from existential reference of even the most indirect, delayed, and ulterior kind. (*Logic*, p. 396)

Within inquiry the function of mathematical propositions is to transform existential ("synthetic") propositions into other such propositions that may be more easily tested empirically (*Logic*, p. 396).

So the early opposition of Peirce to Dewey on the ground that Dewey's "genetic" concept of logic would exclude the kind of logical research that Peirce was doing proves groundless in the light of Dewey's developed position.

Dewey's "logic" incorporates Peirce's critical logic. For Dewey inquiry includes four main stages: the appearance of the problem; the formulation of a hypothesis to solve the problem; the deduction of the consequences of the hypothesis; the testing of the hypothesis by testing the deduced consequences. The last three stages clearly correspond respectively to Peirce's three types of inference: abduction or hypothesis, deduction, and induction. In this way the three aspects of "critical logic" analyzed by Peirce are given their place in inquiry as analyzed by Dewey.[14]

5. *James on Truth*

Inquiry is thought directed to the solution of a problem. It is a basic contention of the pragmatists that a problem always occurs in a context that is unproblematic. Not everything can be problematic (can be "doubted," in the early Peircean formulation) at once. There is thus no general problem of "the existence of the world." Nor is "experience" as such a problem. Thinking human beings living in a world that is more than themselves encounter problems in living in this world. They have developed methods of inquiry to deal with these problems, and for the pragmatist the scientific method is the favored method.

In terms of this attitude, the experienced world is not as such, in its entirety, a matter of "truth" or "knowledge." James, to be sure, did speak of direct experience as "knowledge by acquaintance," but the difference between the direct experience of something and "knowledge about it" proves to be so great that later pragmatists usually restrict "knowledge" (and "truth") to symbolically formulated hypotheses "about" something. Truth and knowledge are then properties of ideas or symbols. What properties? It is useful to begin with James in answering this question, since his orientation is not so directly in terms of inquiry as are those of other pragmatists.

James is forthright in demanding that the pragmatic maxim of meaning be applied to the determination of the meaning of the term "truth."[15] It will be recalled that James interpreted this maxim disjunctively as involving *either* "sensations we are to expect" *or* "reactions we must prepare." We would expect this difference to show up in

59

his views on truth. He begins by admitting that a true idea "agrees" or "corresponds" with reality.[16] The question then becomes what "agrees" or "corresponds" can mean if the pragmatic maxim for meaning is accepted. James further admits that if a sign is a "copy" (an icon), a copy theory of truth is intelligible. But not all signs are icons, and if the logical interpretant is, as Peirce said, a habit, then how can a habit agree or correspond with anything?

James considers a number of ways in which the term "truth" is employed. He finds the prototype of the truth process to be the case where the "leading" of the idea is "simply and fully verified," i.e., the sensations (sensible effects) it leads one to expect do actually occur. A variant of this is where the verification of the leading is partial but not complete.[17] But corresponding to the second aspect of James's version of the pragmatic maxim, there are passages which suggest that an idea is true if the reactions it indicates we are to prepare do turn out to be appropriate to the continuation of the course of action in which we are engaged. These two aspects of his doctrine are brought together in this statement:

> To "agree" in the widest sense with a reality *can only mean to be guided either straight up to it or into its surroundings, or to be put into such working touch with it as to handle either it or something connected with it better than if we disagreed.* Better either intellectually or practically! (*Pragmatism*, pp. 212–13)

When James states that the true is that idea "which gives the maximal combination of satisfactions" (*Essays in Radical Empiricism*, p. 260), he clearly intends to cover both the occurrence of predicted "sensible effects" and the satisfactoriness of the reactions the idea causes us to prepare. Hence it is a travesty of James to say that for him any idea that gives any kind of satisfaction is true. The difficulties that James presents to his reader are that sometimes in fact he brings in "expected sensations" while at other times he seems to be content with the "satisfactoriness" of the reaction which the idea prepares. Thus he can write that "on pragmatic principles we can not reject any hypothesis if consequences useful to life flow from it" (*Pragmatism*, p. 177).

That there is basis for confusion here is clear. The stress on truth as *verified* ideas matches the "expectation-of-sensations" side of his interpretation of the pragmatic maxim while his stress on truth as *satisfactory* ideas tends at times to reflect the consequences-useful-to-life side of his interpretation of that maxim. Thus the two emphases in James's theory of truth reflect the two aspects of his theory of meaning.

Dewey attempted to resolve this confusion in James (and certainly communicated to his readers) in a historically important paper "What Does Pragmatism Mean by Practical?"[18] He argued that in James's treatment of truth there is "a confusion of the test of an idea as idea, with that of the value of a belief as belief." And he claimed that no satisfaction not part of the intent of an idea is relevant to the testing of its truth. James had admitted the same point in a 1907 letter to Arthur O. Lovejoy (in response to Lovejoy's similar criticism), writing that he "sinned" in confusing "consequences of true ideas *per se*, and consequences of ideas *qua believed by us*."[19]

This admission by James, important as it is, could not

wipe out the effects of his earlier writings on truth, nor prevent the often arid controversies which they gave rise to among his critics and adherents. But the issues involved are very subtle, and the situation left by James had at least the merit of raising many important issues for semiotic and the theory of inquiry, such as the conditions under which signs are "accepted," the relation of signification to values, the characteristics of ethical and religious signs. James did not have a sufficiently developed semiotic to talk clearly about such matters, and hence the dangers of confusion of signification and significance, of truth and the acceptance of signs as true, of truth as a value and the value of truth. But his writings helped to force the clarification of such issues. After James it should not be possible to say with a good conscience simply that a true idea "corresponds to the facts."

6. *Peirce and Dewey on Truth*

Peirce and Dewey analyze the term "truth" within the context of inquiry. In Peirce's "The Fixation of Belief" paper, where the scientific method is considered as only one among the possible methods for such "fixation," the concept of truth plays no prominent role:

With the doubt, therefore, the struggle begins, and with the cessation of doubt it ends. Hence the sole object of inquiry is the settlement of opinion. We may fancy that this is not enough for us, and that we seek, not merely an opinion, but a true opinion. But put this fancy to the test, and it proves groundless; for as soon as a firm belief is reached we are entirely satisfied, whether the belief be true or false. (5.375)

This statement indicates that for Peirce the truth of a belief is not to be equated with being "entirely satisfied" with an opinion. What, then, is the truth of a belief?

Peirce's own stress on the scientific method is reflected, as we have seen, in his acceptance of the pragmatic maxim. If, as this maxim states (at least in its earlier formulations), the meaning of an ("intellectual") concept is to be found in the kind of experiences which will be consequent upon a certain kind of action, then the truth of a proposition affirming this concept might simply mean verification that the kind of experience in question is indeed consequent upon the kind of action in question. A true proposition would then be an empirically verified proposition. Such a "verification theory of truth" would fit in with many statements of Peirce, and with many statements of James, Dewey, and Mead. It is certainly a central feature of the pragmatists' doctrine of truth.

But there are complications. For Peirce, since such meanings are general, they can never be completely verified in any particular situation which has occasioned inquiry. So Peirce's emphasis moved away from the stress on inquiry in particular problematic situations to the stress on a continuing process of inquiry by a community of inquirers. A true opinion would then be one which never required revision in the further course of inquiry by the community of inquirers.

This position has raised many problems for Peirce commentators: Is Peirce committed to the position that inquiry will in fact never terminate? Or if it might terminate would the opinions of the "last inquirer" be true? Or if truth be stated in terms of a "limit" of inquiry is the notion of "limit" defensible in this connection? For present purposes we need not discuss these issues;[20] it is sufficient to note that on this analysis of truth one can never be certain that any opinion held at a particular time in a particular situation is "true" (though of course it may be true). This Peirce frankly admits. That this admission does not bother Peirce may be explained by the fact that his characteristic frame of reference is that of the "pure scientists" working in the community of scientists, and accustomed to regard scientific opinions as tentative and subject to correction in the further course of inquiry. But also relevant is the fact that Peirce did not believe that the "vital problems" of life were to be solved by scientific inquiry—but by the "heart" rather than by the "head."[21]

Dewey's approach to inquiry, however, was by way of moral action. Here the focus must be upon the situation, not upon the "long run" of indefinitely continued inquiry— so Dewey focuses upon the relation of inquiry to the specific problematic situation (as do James and Mead). This gives to Dewey's analysis of inquiry a somewhat different (but not incompatible) emphasis than that found in Peirce (especially the later Peirce). We have already noted that Dewey's stress was upon ideas as "plans of action," as judgments of what was to be done to solve the problem posed by a specific situation. Hence if the action was performed and the problem solved, the idea or hypothesis was said to be verified, and to be true.[22] "Truth" in this respect would be situationally determined, a position seemingly at variance with Peirce's view.

Dewey's formulation in the *Logic* removes this apparent discrepancy. He there gives allegiance to Peirce's employment of the term "truth."[23] But since Dewey's stress is still upon inquiry as concerned with the resolution of specific problems, "truth" in this wide sense needs supplementation by something more specific. In fact, in the *Logic* the term "truth" (and the term "knowledge") recedes into the background and stress is laid on the expression "warranted assertion." An assertion is warranted if it is formed on the basis of evidence relevant to a given problem, and if when acted upon the problem occasioning that inquiry is solved. In this connection Dewey employs the term "judgment" rather than "proposition": a judgment is the resolution of a problematic (indeterminate) situation into a nonproblematic (determinate) situation. As already mentioned, the results of the inquiry can be stated in a "proposition," and thus be made available for possible employment in other similar problematic situations.

On Dewey's analysis there is no basic difference, as far as the general process of inquiry is concerned, between scientific inquiry and moral inquiry. Both are held to follow the general pattern of inquiry which Dewey has outlined. What difference there is between them can be clarified only when we have introduced the concept of value.

7. *Rational and Empirical Aspects
of Inquiry: Peirce*

The method of inquiry analyzed by Peirce and Dewey is regarded by them as the method of science and of such common sense inquiries as are the precursors of science. It is also regarded as the method appropriate to a philosophy which accepts the pragmatic maxim. Just as science had by the time of Newton brought both mathematics and experimentation within scientific method, so this generalized theory of inquiry would seem to bring together at the level of philosophy both the "rationalist" and "empiricist" philosophical traditions while avoiding the excesses of each in isolation.[24] Philosophic inquiry would be directed to the solution of experienced problems, and proposed solutions would be tested within the experienced world. But since abduction (or "hypothesis") is not for Peirce induction, bold speculation (together with its deductive elaboration) would be compatible with the acceptance of the pragmatic maxim, provided that the hypotheses proposed be capable of control by empirical observation.

Critics of both Peirce and Dewey have doubted, however, whether their own philosophies do in fact conform to the theory of inquiry they developed and advocated. To the degree that this is so, the criticism may be directed at their philosophies for departing from their professed methodology, or may be directed against their theory of inquiry as being an inadequate expression of what they do in fact maintain as philosophers. Peirce is occasionally viewed as falling within the grip of traditional rationalism (and so as following the "*a priori* method"), while Dewey is alternately viewed as having failed either to get beyond the "subjectivistic" dilemma of the traditional empiricism or beyond the objective idealism of his Hegelian heritage. While I do not think that these accusations are ultimately defensible, it seems worthwhile to consider what there is in the work of Peirce and Dewey that leads to such accusations. Since we do not wish to anticipate the discussion of their "metaphysics"—the topic of a later chapter—we can deal here only with some of the more distinctly methodological issues.

Peirce's "metaphysical rationalism"—insofar as it exists

—stems from his metaphysical confidence in logic and logical analysis. In his earlier work he attempted to go beyond the Kantian logic by formulating logic in terms of semiotic. The laws of logic are then envisaged as the formally necessary principles of semiotic.

There is no doubt, however, but that Peirce tends at times to give metaphysical significance to the results of logical analysis. He finds continuity characteristic of signs (a sign giving rise to a sign which gives rise to a sign, and so on), and so he regards continuity as a characteristic of all that is real. He finds three and only three types of propositions (monadic, dyadic, triadic), and this is taken as evidence of there being only three metaphysical categories. In general Peirce is confident that the developing mind (as a development of signs according to the laws of inference) corresponds to the general development of the cosmos.[25]

Peirce does often write in this "rationalistic" way. And yet this tendency must be qualified in the light of equally insistent statements to the effect that

conceptions which are really products of logical reflection, without being readily seen to be so, mingle with our ordinary thoughts, and are frequently the causes of great confusion. (5.370)

Further, Peirce at times states that continuity is a *methodological* principle[26] (we should seek as much continuity as we can find), even though in most places he writes as if continuity is a general metaphysical principle. It must not be forgotten that Peirce accepted the position of *fallibilism* in his philosophy, so that no matter how convinced he himself was of his metaphysics, he admitted he could not be certain that it was true, i.e., that it would not be subject to modification through further inquiry. In this connection he recognized that phenomenological and scientific application of the three metaphysical categories, which he believed logical analysis had disclosed, might disclose other metaphysical categories.

However "rationalistic" Peirce may seem, or may have been, a dogmatic assertion of his metaphysics would be incompatible with his accepted methodology of inquiry. Peirce is not in intent an *a priori* philosopher in the sense in which in "The Fixation of Belief" he contrasted the *a priori* method to the scientific method. Whether Peirce is always consistent with his intent is another matter.

8. *Rational and Empirical Aspects of Inquiry: Dewey*

With respect to Dewey a common charge has been that his theory of inquiry leads to the skepticism concerning the limits of knowledge which haunted British empiricism. Thus it has been claimed that for Dewey "the world . . . collapses into immediacy." Another and related charge is that Dewey's theory of inquiry leads to an "idealistic" metaphysics in which the "mind" creates in inquiry that which is known.[27]

The ground for these related charges seems to be Dewey's constant stress upon inquiry as involving the *transformation* of a problematic situation into an unproblematic one, so that knowledge has for its object only the situation as transformed—hence it would seem that there is no knowledge of the initial situation prior to its transformation, nor, indeed, of anything which does not issue from such transformation.

Put in another way: Dewey at times defines an object as "an event with meaning." Since inquiry has as its task the constructing of an object in this sense (i.e., a situation no longer problematic, no longer indeterminate in meaning), it would seem that what is known is constructed within inquiry, so that nothing "outside" of inquiry is known.[28] So arises the claim that Dewey is left with only immediate experience and, if inquiry be regarded as "mental," the claim that the "mind" in Dewey's account has created (within immediacy) the object which it knows.

Dewey has replied to such charges many times. He regards his world-view as a "cultural naturalism," in which experience is a part of nature but not all of nature. In his long rejoinder article, "Experience, Knowledge, and Value," in *The Philosophy of John Dewey*[29] (of which P. A. Schilpp was editor), Dewey goes over again the charges that his theory of knowledge is not consistent with his professed naturalistic cosmology. The reader interested in this controversy would do well to consider in detail Dewey's essay. But since the relation of the pragmatic theory of inquiry to the pragmatic cosmology is so central, I would like in the remainder of this section and in the next section, to clarify and perhaps to strengthen some reasons why the pragmatic theory of inquiry is compatible with a naturalistic (or "realistic") cosmology.[30]

A theory of inquiry is an inquiry into inquiry. Hence— as Dewey continually insists—it presupposes other inquiries as the subject-matter for its study. The claim that the problem which occasions an inquiry is set within an unproblematic area is based upon an investigation of these other inquiries—the pragmatist would maintain that claim is a "warranted assertion."

A general theory of inquiry does not in the nature of the case take the place of other specific inquiries. Thus the question as to the age of the earth is to be answered by a specific inquiry into that problem. If a conclusion based on such a specific inquiry is to be challenged, this must be done by further inquiry into the problem—it cannot be settled by a general theory of inquiry. This holds also for such problems as to whether life appeared on the earth which was previously without life, or whether I was born, or whether the world will go on after my death. The answers to such problems cannot be determined by a general theory of inquiry. Even if it is held that a particular inquiry cannot "know" its own antecedents or its own "unproblematic context," these can legitimately be the concern of *other* inquiries—as Dewey specifically contends in the rejoinder referred to. There is no "inquiry-centric predicament" in the pragmatic conception of inquiry.

Why, then, have critics charged Dewey with being committed to a cosmology of "pure immediacy" and often with "idealism" as well? Partly, it would seem, by neglecting the considerations outlined in the two preceding paragraphs. But partly, I believe, because of certain shortcomings in Dewey's formulations of his position.

I do not think that Dewey makes sufficient use of certain resources that the pragmatic position makes eminently available: the social factors in verification on the one hand, and the indirectness of much verification on the other. The point is not that these considerations are completely absent in Dewey's account of knowing, but rather that they are not sufficiently stressed.

If other persons and things are genuinely coordinate in experience with the person who is inquiring—as they are for all four pragmatists—then verification by others of a particular hypothesis should be methodologically on a par with the verification processes of a specific inquirer. Thus the reports by others on my birth may supply the evidence in terms of which I warrantly assert that I was born, even though I cannot make my birth an object of my direct experience.

Such evidence is only a special case of indirect evidence: physical objects may also provide the evidence which warrants assertions by myself or by others.[31] The great bulk of accepted common sense and scientific statements rests upon such indirect evidence. In general any instrument or device (such as the testimony of others and the deliverances of cameras and microscopes) can furnish admissible indirect evidence provided that the reliability of this instrument or device can itself, in other cases, be directly established.

If this be admitted, then acceptance of the general pragmatic theory of inquiry does not in itself dictate the acceptance of such a cosmology as phenomenalism or idealism. There is no incompatibility between Dewey's methodology and his cosmology of cultural naturalism.

9. *Some Aspects of Mead's Conception of an Object*

A situation similar to that discussed in the previous section appears in some interpretations of Mead's thought. Since the issue is important, and since in Mead's case the troublesome problem of the meanings of "object" is brought into prominence,[32] it seems worthwhile to discuss further the relation between pragmatic methodology and pragmatic cosmology.

We have previously noticed that for Mead a "significant symbol" is one which calls out in its producer the same disposition to respond that it calls out in other members of the linguistic community. Thus with such symbols one "takes the role of the other" in the sense that one tends to respond to one's own gestures as others will respond. By an extension of this process one can take the role of physical objects by exciting in oneself the resistance which the object offers to one's pressure upon it. One can in this way symbolically "transcend" one's direct experience by taking the role of other persons and of objects other than persons. Hence it would not be "meaningless" to say that a person can think about the condition of the earth before man appeared or about the different experiences of an object which a person other than himself might undergo. Nor, if the previous statements about indirect evidence are admitted, would there be any objection to saying that such thoughts (as symbolic processes) were "warranted." But in this argument we have been using the expressions "object" and "physical object"; what signification do these terms have for Mead?

Such objects of experience as trees, chairs, and persons, Mead calls "perceptual objects." In any experience some such objects are unproblematic, and are used in the testing of whatever hypothesis appears in a process of inquiry. (Thus for Mead even a theory of perception as developed in psychology presumes perceptual objects for the testing of the theory.)

Such perceptual objects are said to have three kinds of

qualities relative to stages of the action of their perceivers.[33] They have *distance qualities* (colors, seen shapes, etc.), corresponding to activities of the distance senses when the perceiver is not in physical contact with the objects; they have *physical qualities* (measured size, weight, etc.), corresponding to the manipulatory activities of the perceiver; they have *consummatory qualities* ("values") corresponding to the stage of completion of the act in which the perceiver is engaged.

A number of persons may approach a table in the world of their common experience, have different visual perceptions of it and different purposes with respect to it, and yet agree closely on its physical qualities. As beings with significant symbols they can understand the others' communications and establish the similarities of their manipulatory results. When abstraction is made from (the more variable) distance and consummatory properties, there is obtained the "physical object" studied in science.[34]

Now Mead will often write of such physical objects (and indeed of the distance and consummatory qualities of perceptual objects) that they "arise within the act." This is harmless enough when it is remembered that Mead is here working as a social scientist attempting to show how human beings develop the experience and the concept of a physical object. But certain critics of Mead interpret his phrase "within the act" as meaning that the organism literally creates or brings into existence the physical object and that this object has no existence "outside" of such biological acts.[35] Hence they claim that Mead's analysis results in a kind of "biological solipsism."

Certainly nothing was further from Mead's intention, or the general spirit of his work, than such an interpretation. Organism and environment in the form of act and perceptual object are equally basic and in some degree mutually determinative. But Mead never maintained the position that the physical qualities of an object as disclosed under manipulation by an organism are created by that organism.

What, however, is the status of "scientific objects" (such as electrons) which are neither perceptual objects nor abstractions from perceptual objects? Mead suggests that such "scientific objects," and theories about them, can have as their only "meaning" the instrumental function which they serve within scientific inquiry. Thus he writes:

The whole tendency of the natural sciences, as exhibited especially in physics and chemistry, is to replace the objects of immediate experience by hypothetical objects which lie beyond the range of possible experience. As I have pointed out . . . an experimental science must bring any theory to the test of an experience which is immediate, which lies within the "now." It is, in my opinion, a legitimate doctrine . . . that it must be possible to regard the hypothetical subexperiential objects as the statements of the methods and formulas for the control of objects in the world of actual experience, in other words, that so-called objects which lie beyond the range of possible experience are in reality complex procedures in the control of actual experience. (*The Philosophy of the Act*, pp. 291–92)

That such "scientific objects" are "complex procedures in the control of actual experience" is not to be denied; that they are *only* that—as Mead here seems to suggest— is another matter.[36] Mead himself appears at times to be confusing epistemological and cosmological considerations. If the argument in the preceding section is sound, nothing in pragmatism necessitates such a confusion.

10. *Overview of Pragmatic Methodology*

What is most novel in pragmatic methodology is the attempt to deal with the traditional problems of the theory of knowledge within the context of a theory of inquiry. And since inquiry involves the use of symbols, the study of inquiry must make use of semiotic. Hence pragmatic methodology—consonant with the basic emphasis upon a behavioral semiotic—is a semiotically oriented methodology. Knowing is a form of sign behavior, and open to objective inquiry.

The type of inquiry mainly studied (and favored) by the pragmatists is scientific inquiry, which, in a large sense of the term "scientific," is inquiry whose basic terms conform to the requirements of the pragmatic maxim and whose hypotheses are therefore in principle observationally verifiable. The analyses of this type of inquiry given by Peirce and Dewey are in general accord: a problem appears (surrounded by an area of the unproblematic), a hypothesis (abduction) is formed to solve the problem, the consequences of this hypothesis are developed (deduction), and these consequences (and hence the hypothesis) are tested by observation consequent upon acting in terms of these deduced consequences (induction). If the test is positive, the problem disappears and the hypothesis is to that extent verified. The result may then in turn be used as a hypothesis when it seems relevant to new problems which are encountered.

The differences of Peirce and Dewey within this general framework are, however, considerable and important.

75

They relate to the fact that Peirce's orientation is primarily that of a natural scientist while Dewey's orientation is primarily that of a moralist. Peirce tends to stress the indefinite continuation of inquiry; Dewey tends to stress the specific problematic situation which provokes inquiry. Peirce is therefore more concerned with the "truth" of the hypothesis (contingent upon its being sustained indefinitely in further inquiry) while Dewey's stress (though admitting Peirce's "abstract" definition of "truth") is more upon the "warrant" of the assertion with respect to the solution of a specific problem. Both agree that action upon the hypothesis is necessary for verification ("experimentation" in Peirce's large sense), but Dewey's emphasis is upon the actual reconstruction of the situation so that it is no longer problematic. This difference is illustrated in the observational action necessary in studying an eclipse as contrasted in the actual change in the situation in solving a specific moral problem. And the contrast between Peirce as scientist and Dewey as moralist shows up in other ways: Dewey sees little difference between scientific inquiry (in the narrower sense of the term) and moral inquiry; Peirce is doubtful as to the relevance of science in the solution of moral problems.

As to logic, while both Peirce and Dewey agree on the interpretation of logic in the context of inquiry, Peirce's analysis of the laws of logic as laws of semiotic is different (in emphasis at least) from Dewey's analysis of the laws of logic in terms of their status as pragmatic *a priori* principles for the conduct of inquiry.

Both Peirce and Dewey agree that inquiry, while in origin directed to basic human problems of action in problematic situations, may engender problems in its own development. To this extent inquiry becomes "autonomous," and must solve the problems necessary for its own advance. Both would agree in this connection that mathematics is "formal" and "nonexistential in reference," while yet developing within the general framework of inquiry. Peirce, however, regards mathematics as philosophically prior to logic, and puts less stress than Dewey upon its instrumental function within nonmathematical inquiry.

The pragmatic orientation to methodology is able to find a place for both formal reasoning and empirical observation within the process of inquiry, thus avoiding the extremes of traditional "rationalism" and "empiricism." And it differs from Kant's attempted resolution of the conflict by replacing his doctrine of the synthetic *a priori* by the conception of the operational (or pragmatic) *a priori*.

The pragmatists propose that philosophers conform to the pattern of inquiry which has been presented. Whether their own philosophies are always consistent with this proposal is of course another, and disputed, question.

We must next raise the topic of pragmatic axiology. What have the pragmatists to say about values? And does their account of inquiry embrace the solutions of problems concerning values?

NOTES

1. The titles of these articles were: "Questions Concerning Certain Faculties Claimed for Man," "Some Consequences of Four Incapacities," "Grounds of Validity of the Laws of Logic: Further Consequences of Four Incapacities." They are found in the *Collected Papers*, 5.213–357. In these articles Peirce was not centering his attack upon the "substance" aspect of Descartes'

thought, nor was he yet giving his own view of the "psychical" and the "physical." The concern in these articles is solely with the epistemological aspects of Cartesianism. Later discussions of Peirce's conceptions of experience and mind will clarify the grounds for his rejection of this epistemology.

2. *Popular Science Monthly*, 12, 1877, 1–15. Reprinted with later corrections and notes by Peirce in the *Collected Papers*, 5.358–87.

3. Max H. Fisch, "Alexander Bain and the Genealogy of Pragmatism."

4. On Peirce's theory of inquiry and its development see Murray G. Murphey, *The Development of Peirce's Philosophy*.

5. *Popular Science Monthly*, 12, 1878, pp. 286–302. Reprinted in *Collected Papers*, 5.388–410.

6. See Murray G. Murphey, *The Development of Peirce's Philosophy*, pp. 356–64.

7. *Logic*, p. 14, no. 4.

8. This is very clear in the case of Mead. For him a problem is due either to the situation not offering stimulations appropriate to the ongoing of the act or to a conflict between various tendencies to behavior. See his article "A Pragmatic Theory of Truth."

9. The distinction of judgment and proposition, so prominent in Dewey, is not a conventional one and, to me at least, presents difficulties. Hence I have not stressed it in my account. For discussions of the topic see various papers on Dewey by Ernest Nagel in *Sovereign Reason*, especially the paper "Dewey's Reconstruction of Logical Theory." See also H. S. Thayer's *The Logic of Pragmatism*.

10. *Collected Papers*, 8.243–44. The letter is regarded by the editor as having been written about 1905.

11. Dewey himself notes that inquiry involves symbols, so that logical theory involves a theory of symbols (*Logic*, pp. 19–20), but the position is not elaborated in detail.

12. I have not been able to locate this reference.

13. *Logic*, pp. 14, 16. C. I. Lewis earlier had developed a similar position in his conception of the "*pragmatic a priori*," in terms of which he also viewed logical principles as "principles of procedure." The view was presented in his important paper "A Pragmatic Conception of *A Priori*," and developed at length in *Mind and the World Order*. Dewey, surprisingly, does not refer in his *Logic* to Lewis's earlier analysis.

14. Indeed, Peirce himself at times considers the three types of inference *as three stages of inquiry*. Abduction, deduction, and induction are said to be respectively the first, second, and third stages of inquiry. See 6.468–73 (in these paragraphs abduction is called retroduction).

15. The main sources for James's analysis of the term "truth" are the chapter "Pragmatism's Conception of Truth" in his *Pragmatism*, and his book *The Meaning of Truth: A Sequel to "Pragmatism."*

16. *Pragmatism*, pp. 198–200.
17. *Ibid.*, pp. 206–07. This distinction might be compared to C. I. Lewis's distinction between terminating and nonterminating judgments in his book *An Analysis of Knowledge and Valuation*, pp. 184–85, 203–53.
18. *Journal of Philosophy*, 5, 1908, 85–99. This is also printed in Dewey's *Essays in Experimental Logic*. The quotation in the text is from the latter, p. 322n.
19. The letter is quoted in Ralph Barton Perry's *The Thought and Character of William James*, vol. 2, p. 481.
20. See W. V. Quine, *Word and Object*, p. 23. Also "The Pragmatic Theory of Truth" in Edward C. Moore's *American Pragmatism: Peirce, James, and Dewey.*
21. See the 1898 papers which form the concluding chapter of vol. 1 of the *Collected Papers*. The chapter is there entitled "Vitally Important Topics."
22. *Essays in Experimental Logic*, p. 346.
23. *Logic*, p. 345n. James too had admitted (as one use of the term "truth") that "the 'absolutely' true, meaning what no further experience will ever alter, is that ideal vanishing-point towards which we imagine that all our temporary truths will some day converge." To this he added, "meanwhile we have to live today by what truth we can get today, and be ready tomorrow to call it falsehood" (*Pragmatism*, pp. 222–23).
24. See Dewey's analysis of traditional empiricism and rationalism in the concluding chapter of his *Logic*.
25. James does not share Peirce's confidence in the isomorphism of logic and reality: "The most essential features of our mental structure, *viz.*, grammar and logic, *violate* the order of nature as on reflexion we believe it to exist" (quoted in R. B. Perry, *op. cit.*, vol. 1, p. 718).
26. Thus in 6.173 Peirce writes that synechism (the principle of continuity) is not "an ultimate metaphysical doctrine. It is a regulative principle of logic." Charles Hartshorne, in general highly sympathetic to Peirce's thought, thinks that a confusion of possible (or logical) continua with actual continua is Peirce's "most serious mistake." See his article "Charles Peirce's 'One Contribution to Philosophy' and His Most Serious Mistake."
27. As an example of such criticisms see the paper "Dewey's Epistemology and Metaphysics" by Arthur E. Murphy in *The Philosophy of John Dewey*, edited by Paul Arthur Schilpp (2nd ed.), pp. 195–225.
28. Dewey in his *Logic* writes: "The name *objects* will be reserved for subject-matter so far as it has been produced and ordered in settled form by means of inquiry"; "things exist *as* objects only as they have been previously determined as outcomes of inquiries" (p. 119). This is a special employment of the term "object," and not one generally held by pragmatists.
29. *The Philosophy of John Dewey*, pp. 517–608. This article,

written in 1938 as a reply to his critics, should have an important place in the study and evaluation of Dewey's thought.

30. See also my article "Pragmatism and Metaphysics." Also an article by C. I. Lewis, "Some Logical Considerations Concerning the Mental."

31. See Peirce's discussion as to whether the perception of an inkstand may be an hallucination: "If I turn away my eyes, other witnesses will tell me it still remains. If we all leave the room . . . still a photographic camera would show the inkstand still there. . . . Thus or otherwise I confirm myself in the opinion that its characters are what they are, and persist in every opportunity in revealing themselves regardless of what you or I, or any men or generation of men, may think that they are" (8.144).

32. The main sources for Mead's treatment of objects are *The Philosophy of the Act* and *The Philosophy of the Present*.

33. For an introductory statement see "Stages in the Act," pp. 3–25 of *The Philosophy of the Act*.

34. On the "physical thing" see especially *The Philosophy of the Present*, pp. 119–39.

35. See the article by Arthur E. Murphy, "Concerning Mead's *The Philosophy of the Act*."

36. For a development of this position, see Ernest Nagel's discussion of the cognitive status of scientific theories in chapter 6 of his book *The Structure of Science*. Rudolf Carnap agrees with the direction of Nagel's analysis in his *Philosophical Foundations of Physics*.

I V

Pragmatic Axiology

---

1. *Dewey's Central Place in Pragmatic Axiology*

The American pragmatists have all been value-oriented philosophers. At the center of their attention has been man's intelligence-guided goal-seeking activity. Activity has never been regarded by them as mere motion, nor has mere movement ever been extolled by them. They have envisaged life in terms of actions directed to ends or goals, with human life being regarded as distinctive in the degree to which reflective intelligence can guide such actions. While this orientation to value considerations is common to all the major pragmatists, John Dewey is pre-eminently the axiologist of the pragmatic movement. Hence this chapter will center around his thought, bringing in axiological considerations by other pragmatists where they are most relevant.

Dewey has written, in a much quoted passage, that

The problem of restoring integration and cooperation between man's beliefs about the world and his beliefs about the values and purposes that should direct his conduct is the deepest problem of modern life. (*The Quest for Certainty*, p. 255)

Dewey devoted his life as a thinker and as a man to this problem. No one has done this with more tenacity and dedication.

In the statement quoted, Dewey is thinking of "man's beliefs about the world" primarily in terms of these beliefs as affected by science. He sees the historical value orientation of modern man as unsettled by the growth of scientific ideas (and the technology they have helped to support). He sees the general answer to this disorientation to lie not in turning away from science but in its further extension: "Science has hardly been used to modify men's fundamental acts and attitudes in social matters"; "the great scientific revolution is still to come."[1]

In his work on this task Dewey had to develop a general theory of scientific inquiry, and to show in the light of this theory that value-problems were amenable to such inquiry. He has applied his general methodological and axiological orientation to such special fields as ethics, social philosophy, education, aesthetics, religion, and philosophy itself.

The total work is certainly one of the major contributions of a modern philosopher to modern life. Mead held that "in the profoundest sense John Dewey is the philosopher of America."[2] Dewey was introduced in 1920 at the National University of Peking as "the second Confucius." Whitehead wrote that Dewey "is the chief intellectual force providing that environment [the North American continent] with coherent purpose."[3] And in recent years especially there have been criticisms as virulent as such praises are high. Dewey as axiologist and as moralist is clearly a man to be reckoned with.

2. *The Subject-Matter of Pragmatic Axiology*

In keeping with their general orientation, the pragmatists can be expected to develop a theory of value which links values to action, which regards distinctively value terms (such as "good" and "ought" in their most distinctive occurrences) as analyzable in terms of the general pragmatic view of meaning, and which maintains that evaluations (as inquiries into what objects or actions are to be valued) are amenable to the same general pattern of inquiry which occurs in science.

Dewey deals with all these issues in detail. We will use as the main sources for his views his monograph *Theory of Valuation*[4] and the pages on evaluation in his *Logic*. Dewey never systematized his axiology in one large work as the *Logic* did for his methodology, but the monograph *Theory of Valuation* gives at least the essential points of his axiological position. In this monograph (p. 5) he employs the terms *prizing* and *appraising* to mark an important distinction:

When attention is confined to the usage of the verb "to value," we find that common speech exhibits a double usage. For a glance at the dictionary will show that in ordinary speech the words "valuing" and "valuation" are verbally employed to designate both *prizing*, in the sense of holding precious . . . and *appraising* in the sense of *putting* a value upon, *assigning* value to. . . .

83

In Dewey's *Logic* he employs the terms "enjoy" and "evaluate" to mark the same distinction.

Prizing (or enjoying), then, is a kind of preferential action or behavior[5] toward something (actual or ideal), and common speech often calls that which is prized or enjoyed "a value." Appraising (or evaluation), in contrast, would be the conclusion as a result of inquiry that something actual or ideal is worthy of prizing or should be prized. The relation of prizing and appraisal is reciprocal: when what to prize has become a problem, inquiry would be directed to solving this problem, i.e., to determine what should be prized, and the resulting appraisal would then determine a new prizing or confirm an existing one. Such appraisive inquiry, like all inquiry, would occur within an area of the unproblematic, in this case an area of unproblematic prizings. So conceived, axiology would be the study of prizings and appraisals, and their relationship; it would have an empirical subject-matter, and it would bring the study of appraisals (or evaluations) within the general theory of inquiry. Axiology so conceived may be regarded as the distinctive feature of pragmatic axiology.

Nevertheless, this account as given is somewhat too simple to be an exact presentation of Dewey's view, and in any case it bristles with problems. To these matters we must now turn.

3. *Further Consideration of Dewey's Axiology*

If the basic empirical phenomenon of value is located in relation to such behavior as prizing or enjoying, it would

seem natural to define "value" in the widest sense as anything insofar as it is prized or enjoyed. James moves in
this direction: in his essay "The Moral Philosopher and
the Moral Life"[6] he wrote: *The essence of good is simply
to satisfy demand.*" Ralph Barton Perry, whose "interest
theory of value" took off from this essay of James, defined
in his *General Theory of Value*[7] generic value as "any
object of any interest." C. I. Lewis, looking for an empirical base for the meaning of the phrase "the immedi-
ately valuable" found it in the "prizings and disprizings
of the presently given content of experience."[8] Dewey himself preferred not to apply the term "value" to everything
prized,[9] but only to those cases where something is prized
after envisaging the consequences of prizing it. A value
in this restricted sense, while not necessarily the result
of a full-fledged appraisal or evaluation, requires at least
a minimal "intellectual" process of anticipation of consequences. In *The Quest for Certainty* Dewey defines "value"
by "enjoyments which are the consequences of intelligent
action" (p. 259).

The issue of the wisdom (and precise boundary) of
this restriction of the term "value" is arguable,[10] but
attention has been called to this matter here only because
of the importance of the question whether Dewey's view
has a place for a "value unproblematic" which surrounds
every evaluation and sets the limits within which an
inquiry concerning values has its solution. The answer
is "no" if every value which functions in terminating an
inquiry is determined in that inquiry, and "yes" if this is
not the case. What is Dewey's position on this point?

Dewey clearly does not want values imported into inquiry but to be "determined in and by the process of
inquiry" (*Logic*, p. 503). He is insistent that the validity

or warrantness of an evaluation is relative to a particular problematic situation. The results of previous evaluations are, of course, relevant to the solution of a particular value problem, just as the solutions of previous scientific inquiries are relevant to the solution of a specific scientific problem. But in both cases they are for Dewey relevant only as *instruments* for forming hypotheses concerning the resolution of a given problem, and are not *standards* in terms of which a judgment is made or tested. The "ends-in-view" with respect to a given problematic situation *are formed in that situation*, and their test is whether they solve the particular problem of that situation. So in a sense in Dewey's view there seems to be an unproblematic context for every inquiry, but no specifically "value unproblematic" context for evaluative inquiry.

On the other hand, Dewey is quite specific in maintaining that "we evaluate only when a value, in the sense of material enjoyed, has become problematic" (*Logic*, p. 172). He is equally specific that "that which limits [an evaluation] never is judged in the particular situation in which it is limiting." He at times calls this unjudged factor the "invaluable," but adds:

The word does not mean something of supreme value as compared with other things any more than it means something of zero value. . . . It means, in short, that judgment at some point runs against the brute fact of holding something dear as its limit. (*Essays in Experimental Logic*, p. 384)

It seems, then, that whether or not the term "value" is applied to the object of any prizing, the point remains that evaluation, as determining what to prize, occurs in a problematic situation which includes unproblematic prizings, and that these provide (at least part of) the context in which hypotheses as to what to prize are tested. So conceived, evaluations are genuine "cognitive" judgments, empirical in nature and capable of experimental testing in situations in which some prizings are unproblematic. This I take to be central in pragmatic axiology.

4. Relation of Evaluation to the General Theory of Inquiry

The preceding discussion would suggest that evaluation follows the same general process of inquiry as does scientific thinking. To show this was one of the major goals of Dewey's philosophy. To the extent that Dewey has established this point, the whole field of human value problems lies open for the employment of the same general method of inquiry that has had such dramatic success in science. There are, however, in Dewey's defense of this position certain qualifications to be made, and certain ambiguities to be resolved.

We saw in the chapter on pragmatic semiotic that Dewey quite early admitted a distinction between "judgments of fact," "judgments of good," and "judgments of practice," but tended to subordinate the first two to the latter: judgments of fact and judgments of good were held to occur only in a context requiring judgments of practice and to serve as instruments for judgments of practice. But the analysis of the nature of, and the relations between, these three forms of judgment leaves much to be desired in Dewey's early writings.

Nor does the *Logic* entirely clarify the issues that are involved. The distinction between judgments of good and judgments of practice—never stressed much by Dewey[11]—seems not to be made here. It is true that the term "appraisal" (or "estimate") is frequently employed in describing the course of inquiry, but it is limited to the "partial judgments" involved in moving toward the final judgment of practice which is the solution of the problem generating inquiry (*Logic*, pp. 133, 140). Whether these "partial judgments" are or are not regarded as preliminary judgments of practice does not seem to me to be clear.

However, in the *Logic* "judgments of fact" (now called "declarative or enunciative propositions") are much in evidence. But they too are regarded as "instrumentalities" needed in the course of inquiry. Hence there would seem to be only one type of inquiry, namely, that issuing in judgments of practice. And it might be thought that this is what Dewey understands by pragmatism.

There are other strains in Dewey's writings that would not seem to necessitate the view that inquiry as such always terminates in a judgment of practice. He admits that inquiry involves investigations to determine what the "facts" are (the existential conditions present or past) so that inquiry may proceed. I see no reason why such investigations might not be called inquiries (or subinquiries), nor why their conclusions should be called judgments of practice.

For example, even if the inquiry into cancer, as a total human enterprise, arises from the problems posed to human life by cancer, it seems doubtful if we would (or should) describe the conclusions of subinquiries into whether particular substances are cancerigenic as judgments of practice (i.e., judgments as to what should be done). It is true that we will prize certain substances and disprize others as a result of these (sub) inquiries, but the declaration that a given substance is or is not cancerigenic seems to have no relation to human prizing either in its signification or its mode of confirmation. Hence this particular inquiry (or subinquiry) does not seem to eventuate in a judgment of practice.

In the light of these considerations, it might be wise to distinguish (in the manner of Kant) problems of what to believe to be the case, problems of what to prize, and problems of what to do. The inquiries devoted to these problems *eventuate* in different types of symbolic expressions. In this way we might distinguish designative, appraisive, and prescriptive inquiries.[12] That all of these types of inquiry may in Dewey's wide sense of the term become "scientific," would merely mean that they might come to exemplify the general pattern of inquiry which Dewey has analyzed and which historically has been most clearly manifested in the work of scientists. And this would be compatible with the recognition that the subtypes of inquiry do differ among themselves in the type of problems they deal with and in the symbolic expressions in which they eventuate. Such recognition would protect Dewey from the charge of "scientism" often (and I think wrongly) leveled at him by critics.[13] It would also protect him from the opposite charge that his general theory of inquiry is biased by his own ethical orientation[14] and so is not "scientific" enough

5. *The Problem of Axiological Disciplines*

If general axiology is centered on the empirical phenomena of prizing and the type of inquiry that issues in evaluations ("judgments of good" and "judgments of ought"), then specific axiological disciplines might be systematically distinguished in terms of specific types of prizings, and consequently in terms of the specific "value unproblematics" which are involved in the corresponding specific evaluations. A comprehensive and systematic pragmatic axiology would encompass this task. No such systematic pragmatic axiology exists.[15]

It is true that Peirce had a specific subdivision of normative sciences in philosophy, and held that logic was dependent on ethics, and ethics was dependent on aesthetics. But this was a late phase of Peirce's work and remains fragmentary;[16] nor was it oriented in the manner of our previous suggestion. Dewey did not attempt to relate his general axiology (insofar as it is foreshadowed in his *Theory of Valuation*) to his treatments of such specific fields as ethics and aesthetics. Nevertheless, the pragmatists have been greatly concerned with specific fields of value, and we shall consider some of their ideas about ethics, political theory, aesthetics, and religion.[17]

One general observation must first be made. On the pragmatic orientation it would be necessary in all cases to find the empirical subject-matter of the discipline in question. And then it would be important to distinguish the general theoretical issues involved in each discipline from the specific evaluations which a particular pragmatist might hold. For example, theoretical ethics would be concerned with such problems as delimiting the field of moral problems and of determining what is meant by calling an act "morally right"—as distinct from the evaluation of a certain act in a specific situation as morally right. Similar distinctions would be necessary in other axiological fields. Two pragmatists might agree on the general nature of axiology and the delimitations of the special axiological disciplines and yet disagree on specific evaluations—as Mead and Dewey differed on whether the United States should join the League of Nations set up after World War I, or as James and Peirce differed in their emphases upon the importance of the individual and the community.

6. *Pragmatic Ethics*

Ethics is the theory of moral behavior. What then is moral behavior? Philosophers have differed in their answers: some philosophers would regard all problems of prudence as moral problems, while others would not. I believe that all pragmatists have thought of moral behavior in social terms. To consider the behavior of an individual person from a moral point of view would be to consider this behavior as it affects other persons as well as the individual himself. Moral evaluation would then be inquiry directed to determining morally right (or wrong) behavior.

As the preceding pages would suggest, it is characteristic of the pragmatic ethical orientation to consider moral problems in terms of specific and unique situations.[18] Thus James, holding that "the essence of good is to satisfy a demand," took the moral task to be the realization of as much good as possible in situations in which "demands" conflict:

There is but one unconditional commandment, which is that we seek incessantly, with fear and trembling, so to vote and to act as to bring about the very largest total universe of good which we can see. . . . Every real dilemma is in literal strictness a unique situation; and the exact combination of ideals realized and ideals disappointed which each decision creates is always a universe without a precedent, and for which no adequate previous rule exists.[19]

Similarly, relating value to the consummatory phase of action, Mead writes:

The moral question is not one of setting up a right value over against a wrong value; it is a question of finding the possibility of acting so as to take into account as far as possible all the values involved (*The Philosophy of the Act*, p. 465). We have no more right to neglect a real value than we have to neglect a fact in a scientific problem. In the solution of a problem we must take all relevant values into account. (*Ibid.*, p. 461)[20]

The stress upon "the unique situation" in which moral behavior and moral evaluation occur and are tested, is especially prominent in Dewey's ethical theory. It is prominent, for instance, in his chapter on morality in *Reconstruction in Philosophy* as well as in his *Theory of Valuation*. The determination of what is right to do (of what should be done morally) is, like all evaluations, determined by finding what is required in the resolution of a specific problematic situation. The specific moral hypothesis is formed in the situation and not imported into it:

Ends-in-view are appraised or valued as *good* or *bad* on the ground of their serviceability in the direction of behavior dealing with states of affairs found to be objectionable because of some lack or conflict in them. They are appraised as fit or unfit, proper or unproper, *right* or *wrong*, on the ground of their *requiredness* in accomplishing this end. (*Theory of Valuation*, p. 47)

It is a frequent criticism of such "situationism" in ethical (and also in political) theory that it has no place for accumulated moral knowledge and wisdom. But for Dewey this is certainly not the case:

Generalized ideas of ends and value undoubtedly exist. They exist not only as expressions of habit and as uncritical and probably invalid ideas, but also in the same way as valid general ideas arise in any subject. . . . As with general ideas in the conduct of any natural science, these general ideas are used as intellectual instrumentalities in judgment of particular cases as the latter arise; they are, in effect, tools that direct and facilitate examination of things in the concrete while they are also developed and tested by the results of their application in these cases. (*Theory of Valuation*, p. 44)

In the historically important volume *Ethics*, written by Dewey and James II. Tufts,[21] a distinction was made between "reflective" and "customary" morality. What we have been concerned with in these pages would be in those terms reflective morality. But as the last quotation made clear, general moral ends and principles are not denied. These would include "customary" moral principles. Neither their validity nor their instrumentality is necessarily denied. At least some of them might even be regarded as "operationally *a priori*" in the sense in which that label has previously been used. But they would still be considered as arising out of concern with specific moral problems, and as being controlled by their aid in meeting further specific moral problems.

7. *Political Theory: Democracy as a Moral Conception*

In any process of direct social interaction—moral or not—the interactions of the persons directly involved have effects upon other persons, and these other persons constitute a "public." In any process of direct social interaction there is a "public" composed of persons other than those in direct interaction, but affected by the interaction. Every member of a social community is in fact part of the public, relative to the direct social interactions of other members of the community. The members of a social community, as a public, develop rules or norms or standards of social interaction applicable to all members of the community in order to control the public effects of social interaction. Insofar as these are maintained by force they constitute a set of laws; the persons to whom these laws are applicable are members of a political community; and the persons who enforce the laws constitute a government. Political theory is the general study of political communities.

The previous paragraph is a rather free rendering of Dewey's position in his book *The Public and Its Prob-*

lems.[22] It is here presented as a background for Dewey's interpretation of, and relation to, American democracy.

It is evident at once to the reader of *The Public and Its Problems*, and related works,[23] that Dewey is not writing as a political scientist attempting to describe the political institutions of the United States. Dewey writes rather as one committed to American democracy, very critical of much that he found around him in its workings but concerned with its improvement and extension. Dewey does not define democracy in terms of historical, political, or economic institutions. Democracy for Dewey was basically a *moral conception.*

This is evident as early as 1888 in a paper delivered at the University of Michigan with the title "The Ethics of Democracy." Democracy was there envisaged as *the acceptance of the moral method of dealing with all social problems.* The moral method as he later interpreted it in detail, was, as we have seen, the application of inquiry (essentially as found in science) to the solution of value problems arising in social situations. Democracy, in Dewey's conception, would extend this moral orientation to political problems—political problems then become moral problems. Since for Dewey in the solution of any value problem the end-in-view is to be formed in terms of the means available, and the means available are to be appraised in terms of their suitability to the emerging ends-in-view (so that the choice of means and the end-in-view are simultaneously decided), moral action—and hence in this extension, political action—must use moral means for the attempted attainment of moral ends.[24]

Another way of expressing this position is to say that for Dewey (and James and Mead) the moral point of view considers each person in a problematic value situation as an end and never merely as a means—a formulation that shows the affiliation of this position with the Kantian, and hence Christian, heritage. The extension of this position to the problems of the entire community would be the acceptance of democracy as a moral conception.

One additional point should be stressed since it bears on one of the most distinctive contributions of American pragmatism. Peirce, with his orientation to the scientific community and its social process of inquiry, tended to disparage individuality. James, in contrast, with his stress on particular persons, glorified the individual: after agreeing that "the group is inferior to the individual," he wrote: "Let us be content to demand of democracy that it shall not stifle the individual. That is everything."[25]

With Dewey and Mead, however, the individual and the social community become completely correlative. Dewey wrote that the individual is "the reconstructive center of society." With Mead he agrees that the reflective, self-conscious moral individual arises only in a social process, but that only such an individual in turn makes possible the more complex and distinctive levels of human society. So for Dewey and Mead human society is neither a mosaic of independent individuals nor an organic whole in which the individual is merged. Thus their conception of democracy is at odds both with the advocates of "laissez faire" and of "totalitarian" political systems. It seems to me that this recognition of the complete mutuality of the individual and the social is one of the most important achievements of the pragmatic movement.

8. *Aesthetics and the Aesthetic Aspect of Experience*

There is no better evidence of the falsity of the common popular interpretation of pragmatism as a philosophy of "practicality," "opportunism," and "scientism" than the high place accorded to aesthetic experience (and hence to art and artists) by the American pragmatists. Indeed, there is a sense in which emphasis upon the aesthetic aspect of experience is the culmination of this philosophic movement.

Although the literature on pragmatic aesthetics is not extensive, no adequate presentation is possible in a few pages.[26] Attention will be focused upon Dewey's views, since his work (especially *Art as Experience*) is of central importance for this topic.

Dewey wrote, in *Reconstruction in Philosophy*:

Surely there is no more significant question before the world than the question of the possibility and method of reconciliation of the attitudes of practical science and contemplative esthetic appreciation.[27]

Art as Experience, published in 1934 (fourteen years later), gives Dewey's answer to this question. In this work Dewey directs attention to what is involved in the everyday practice of speaking of "*an* experience":

We have *an* experience when the material experienced runs its course to fulfillment. Then and then only is it integrated within and demarcated in the general stream of experience from other experiences. A piece of work is finished in a way

97

that is satisfactory; a problem receives its solution; a game is played through; a situation, whether that of eating a meal, playing a game of chess, carrying on a conversation, writing a book, or taking part in a political campaign, is so rounded out that its close is a consummation and not a cessation. Such an experience is a whole and carries with it its own individualizing quality and self-sufficiency. It is *an* experience. (*Art as Experience*, p. 35)

In a distinctively esthetic experience, characteristics that are subdued in other experiences are dominant; those that are subordinate are controlling—namely, the characteristics in virtue of which the experience is an integrated complete experience on its own account. (*Ibid.*, p. 55)

An object is peculiarly and dominantly esthetic, yielding the enjoyment characteristic of esthetic perception, when the factors that determine anything which can be called *an* experience are lifted high above the threshold of perception and are made manifest for their own sake. (*Ibid.*, p. 57)

When aesthetic experience is characterized in this way, it becomes clear that the aesthetic is not one special kind of experience sharply differentiated from other kinds of experience, but that it is a question of the degree to which an experience takes on a consummatory character. To the extent that this is so experience is aesthetic, and such experience is the subject-matter of aesthetics. Art is only a part of this subject-matter, for art as a human product may be regarded as the production of objects specifically formed to permit and sustain aesthetic experience.

Since the production and the perception of a work of art are human activities (and for Dewey quite similar human activities) and since having an aesthetic experience, even when not instigated by a work of art, involves

98

the consummatory phase of activity, the whole of Dewey's aesthetics is consonant with the actional orientation of pragmatism. Nor is even the "instrumental" aspect of Dewey's thought lost in this analysis. For the works produced by artists may be regarded as ways of changing and supplementing man's environment so that he extends his control over the consummatory aspects of his experience.

Where, then, does the "contemplative" element in "aesthetic appreciation" come in? Dewey has at his command at least two resources relevant at this point. One is his recognition that experience is two-sided: it is a matter of "undergoing" as well as of "doing." What one undergoes as a result of doing can itself be reacted to and become an object of (or a component of) aesthetic experience. Dewey's own dominant orientation is so strongly that of a moralist that he does not always in his writings adequately stress the "undergoing" aspect of experience—but this neglect is corrected in his aesthetics.

More importantly, Dewey has available for his aesthetics the general pragmatist emphasis upon semiotic. While it is not necessary that it always be done, it is possible to signify "*an* experience," and thus to gain a kind of contemplative attitude toward it. But of greater significance is the fact that even if not all works of art are signs (and this is a disputed point) many of them admittedly are signs or contain signs.

Dewey in *Art as Experience* has much to say concerning the "meaning" of a work of art, especially in the chapter "The Expressive Object." He does this by distinguishing between expression and statement: "Science states meanings; art expresses them" (p. 84). Some clarification of this distinction is given in the following passage:

99

The poetic as distinct from the prosaic, esthetic art as distinct from scientific, expression as distinct from statement, does something different from leading to an experience. It constitutes one. A traveler who follows the statement or direction of a signboard finds himself in the city that he has been pointed towards. He may then *have* in his own experience some of the meaning which the city possesses. He may have it to such an extent that the city has expressed itself to him— as Tintern Abbey expressed itself to Wordsworth in and through his poem. . . . Wordsworth's poem is different from the account of Tintern Abbey given by an antiquarian. The poem . . . does not operate in the dimension of correct descriptive statement but in that of experience itself. Poetry and prose, literal photograph and painting, operate in different media to distinct ends. Prose is set forth in propositions. The logic of poetry is super-propositional even when it uses what are, grammatically speaking, propositions. The latter have intent; art is an immediate realization of intent. (*Art as Experience*, p. 85)

While Dewey does not use Peirce's semiotical terminology, it can be seen from this quotation (and from his frequent references to paintings in *Art as Experience*) that the work of art often, and perhaps always, may be regarded as an iconic sign—a notion that plays a central place in Peirce's scattered but suggestive remarks about aesthetics.[28] The peculiarity of an iconic sign is that what it signifies is embodied in the sign vehicle itself; hence if it signifies a consummatory experience something of that consummatory experience is embodied in the sign vehicle itself—and so is "contemplated" in the experience of the sign.[29] This is not the full story of how Dewey's concept of "expressive meaning" might be interpreted, but it does illustrate that resources of semiotic are available for the elucidation of Dewey's concept.

9. *Religion and Human Values*

"Religion," James wrote, "whatever it is, is a man's total reaction upon life."[30] James did not himself think this was a sufficient criterion of religion, nor would Peirce. For both of them additional beliefs would be involved (as of higher divine powers with which one could cooperate in the conduct of life). But for James these specifically religious beliefs differed widely between individuals and cultures and so were in a sense secondary to the common religious function of furnishing man a "total reaction upon life."

Although none of the pragmatists wrote as, or had kind words for, traditional theologians, they were without exception sympathetic to the general role that religion played in human life. Peirce and James held beliefs nearest to the traditional theological content of Christianity; Mead and Dewey viewed religion in naturalistic terms. Since it is impossible to deal with the position of all these men on religion in this chapter, we will focus here, somewhat arbitrarily, on Mead's thought.[31]

Mead believed that certain assumptions of Christianity "have been of very great importance in the history of the Western world" (*The Philosophy of the Act*, p. 466). One of these assumptions was that of the intelligibility of the world. This helped to give to Western man confidence in his intellectual enterprises—philosophic and scientific. Other doctrines, such as the fatherhood of God and the brotherhood of man, helped to give man confidence in his practical enterprises, and played a part in the movement toward political democracy.

Mead distinguished two aspects of the religious experience itself: the "mystical" aspect and "the need for salvation." He attempted to characterize both of these in terms of his social psychology.

The mystical aspect of the religious experience—"that attitude of feeling at one with everybody and everything about us" (*Mind, Self, and Society*, p. 275)—he regarded as the complete generalization of role-taking to persons and things:

> One's interest is the interest of all. There is complete identification of individuals. Within the individual there is the fusion of the "me" with the "I." (*Ibid.*, p. 274). The social situation is spread over the entire world. (*Ibid.*, p. 275)

The "need for salvation" Mead regarded as the more important of the two aspects of the religious experience, and he dealt with it at greater length (*The Philosophy of the Act*, pp. 475–78). He regarded the need as "not the salvation of the individual but the salvation of the self as a social being" (p. 476). As social selves, according to Mead, "we always carry ideals of a social order which is not found in the conditions under which we live" (p. 475). The greater the discrepancy, the greater is the need for social change, and the more widespread is the need for salvation (see p. 477). "Our religious experiences come back to that possibility of the development of society so as to realize those values which belong to social beings" (p. 476). He asks rhetorically the question: "Is not the great genius in the field of religion one who in a certain sense carries in himself a higher social order and so transcends his immediate one?" (p. 477).

It is to be noted that Mead does not supplement this

social-psychological interpretation of the religious experience with a religious metaphysics of the sort found in
Peirce and James:

There is no way at the present time that we can with any
security connect the history of man and the values which have
appeared in society with the history of the physical universe.
(*The Philosophy of the Act*, p. 478)

Nor does Mead look to theology to ground the evaluations
needed to meet individual and social problems. He deals
with these issues in his paper "Experimentalism as a Philosophy of History" (*The Philosophy of the Act*, pp. 494–
519).

In this essay Mead contrasts "the Augustinian philosophy of history" in which "all values were authoritatively
defined and fixed" with "the new philosophy of history,
that of social evolution" (p. 504). In this "new philosophy
of history," which Mead obviously favors, man meets his
social problems as they appear. Mead admits that some
remaking of values "takes place . . . far below the
threshold of reflective experience" (p. 504). But he, in
harmony with the pragmatic ethical theory which we have
already discussed, believes that the *method* of science
should now be used in facing our social problems (p. 509).
Mead is very clear that the stress is upon the application
of the scientific method and not in asking scientists or
"science" "what to do." Neither metaphysics, nor theology,
nor science can substitute for the activity of moral evaluation.

If one's philosophy of history is of the evolutionary sort,
one finds the meaning of life in marshaling all the values that

are involved in the problems of conduct and interpretation, and seeking such a reconstruction of them as will motivate conduct that recognizes all the interests that are involved. (*The Philosophy of the Act*, p. 512)

In conclusion, it may be said that while all of the pragmatists are sympathetic to certain features of religion, and while Peirce and James—unlike Mead and Dewey—themselves held a form of Christian theology, the characteristic emphasis of pragmatism has been upon religion as a factor in the total orientation of man rather than upon religion as a system of theological beliefs.

10.   *Overview of Pragmatic Axiology*

The contribution of the American pragmatists to the theory of value is one of their major philosophical achievements. Dewey's commanding place in this area is evident. James's work is also value-oriented and is of special importance for the topic of religion, but he does not deal with the more technical axiological issues, nor the diversity of axiological subject-matters, in the way that Dewey does. And while Peirce's whole philosophy is permeated with notions of value, his specific dealing with axiological matters came late in his life and was more concerned with the place of the normative sciences in the architectonic of his philosophy than with the detailed analysis of value terms and evaluations. Mead's conception of the consummatory stage of the act, and his analysis of role-taking, are of great relevance to axiological problems, but the exhibition of this relevance was not at the center of his interest. Dewey stands forth as the pre-eminent axiologist of the movement. Hence our concern was primarily with his thought.

What the pragmatists have in common in their approach to the theory of value is their location of values within the context of a living being in relation to its world, and the placing of evaluation within their general theory of inquiry. Axiology is thus empirically and behaviorally oriented.

Values as observational phenomena are isolated with respect to behavior, however this is done in detail: as that which is or would be experienced as "admirable" (Peirce); as the properties of an object which permit the consummation of an act (Mead); as the satisfaction of "demands" (James); as the objects of prizings, or more narrowly, of those prizings which occur after the anticipation of the consequences of such prizing (Dewey).

Common to these views is the conception that action is "purposive" or "telic" or "goal-oriented"—terms whose applications are intended to be capable of observational confirmation. This does not imply that in all actions the "end" is an "end-in-view." With respect to a dog that is "going home," his impulses are such that only a certain situation will permit their overt completion, and his movements are such as tend to bring him to this situation. This does not require that the end of getting home is for the dog an end-in-view, i.e., that it signifies this goal and that such signifying determines (at least in part) its actual movements. Much of human behavior (though by no means all) does have its end symbolically in view.

Evaluation is seen (especially by Dewey) as inquiry to determine what is to be prized in a value-problematic situation, that is, in a situation in which prizing has become problematic. Such inquiry forms through deliberation an end-in-view, and the testing of this in terms of its ability to solve the problem it is intended to solve. Evaluative inquiry can be (and for Dewey, should be) of the same general type of inquiry found in science; its difference lies in the type of problem (i.e., a value or prizing problem) which is its occasion. Similarly, there can be special types of value-problems, and their differences would reflect the differences of evaluation in inquiries primarily ethical or political or aesthetical in nature.

All such inquiries will in any specific case take place within an unproblematic context, that is, unproblematic for that situation. The results of various successful inquiries will give rise to a body of knowledge (warranted assertions for Dewey) that like all generalizations will be used as tools (not as dogmas) for approaching new value-problems.

There is considerable agreement in the general unproblematic values of the various pragmatists themselves —they are "for" scientific method, democracy, morality. This, of course, does not prevent certain differences among them. And this is understandable if we distinguish between a person's general theory of the nature of values and evaluations and his own personal values and evaluations.

The main technical difficulties in the pragmatic axiology seem to me to lie in the fact that the pragmatists do not develop and apply a common semiotic to the analysis of axiological and nonaxiological terms and sentences. Hence it is not easy to be sure of the relation of "judgments of fact," "judgments of good," and "judgments of practice" to each other or to the pragmatic maxim. At times the last two judgments are distinguished from each other and at times they are not. Nor is the relation of one or both of these to "judgments of fact" always clear. As a result the relation of axiological to nonaxiological inquiry becomes ambiguous. We have noted earlier that pragmatic semiotic—important as it is—remained incomplete in its development, and this incompleteness manifests itself anew in the pragmatic version of axiology.

That evaluations have a genuine "cognitive content" or "intellectual purport" (and are not merely expressions of emotions or attempts to influence others) is an important feature of pragmatic axiology. This doctrine is held in common by all the pragmatists. It is central to their entire enterprise.

NOTES

1. John Dewey, *The Quest for Certainty*, pp. 324, 329.
2. G. H. Mead, "The Philosophies of Royce, James, and Dewey, in their American Setting." The sentence quoted is the final sentence of the article.
3. In "John Dewey and His Influence," in *The Philosophy of John Dewey*, edited by Paul Arthur Schilpp (2nd ed.), p. 478.
4. This appeared as monograph 4, vol. 2, of the *International Encyclopedia of Unified Science*. An important late paper is Dewey's "The Field of 'Value'" in *Value: A Cooperative Inquiry*, edited by Ray Lepley.
5. This is a term I have employed. Dewey very seldom uses the term "preference" in this connection; his favored expression (at least late in his life) was "selective-rejective behavior" (see the article in the Lepley volume referred to in the preceding note). Nor did Dewey himself use the term "axiology"; "theory of valuation" is his general term and embraces both the study of prizings and appraisals (or evaluations).
6. *The International Journal of Ethics*, 1, 1891, pp. 330–54.
7. This book is supplemented by Perry's *Realms of Value*. These

two works form one of the major contributions to modern axiology.

8. *An Analysis of Knowledge and Valuation*, p. 397. The term "value" when applied to an object implied for Lewis "some potentiality of it for satisfaction in experience" (p. 528).

9. Cf. Peirce's denial that "the mere satisfaction of an impulse can be said to be *per se* a good, at all" (1.583).

10. See my paper "Axiology as the Science of Preferential Behavior," in *Value: A Cooperative Inquiry*, edited by Ray Lepley, pp. 211–22.

11. For statements by Dewey on the difference between "good" and "right," see his *Theory of Valuation*, pp. 47, 57.

12. See my book *Signification and Significance: A Study of the Relations of Signs and Values*.

13. Dewey's stress on "science" is primarily a stress on the "scientific attitude." He writes about this as follows: "The scientific attitude is here conceived as a quality that is manifested in any walk of life. What, then, is it? On its negative side, it is freedom from control by routine, prejudice, dogma, unexamined tradition, sheer self-interest. Positively, it is the will to inquire, to examine, to discriminate, to draw conclusions only on the basis of evidence after taking pains to gather all available evidence. It is the intention to reach beliefs, and to test those that are entertained, on the basis of observed facts, recognizing also that facts are without meaning save as they point to ideas. It is, in turn, the experimental attitude which recognizes that while ideas are necessary to deal with facts, yet they are working hypotheses to be tested by the consequences they produce" (*Theory of Valuation*, p. 31).

14. Dewey is aware of the possibility of this charge, and says if he were to turn critic of his views he would make this charge—in order to refute it. (See his Rejoinder in *The Philosophy of John Dewey*, edited by Paul Arthur Schilpp, pp. 579 ff.)

15. The previously mentioned book by Ralph Barton Perry, *Realms of Value*, may be regarded as an important contribution to this task.

16. See *Charles S. Peirce: On Norms and Ideals*, by Vincent G. Potter.

17. A short paper on "John Dewey as Educator" is included in the Appendix.

18. This would seem not to hold for Peirce, whose stress is more upon following "customary morality" than upon the solution of a moral problem by reflective inquiry.

19. William James, "The Moral Philosopher and the Moral Life," pp. 349–50.

20. Mead's main paper on ethics is "Scientific Method and the Moral Sciences." Mead's theory of role-taking makes it possible to awaken in oneself the value-attitudes of other persons, so there is no value-egocentric predicament for him just as there is no

epistemological-egocentric predicament. For Mead's view of value in relation to the consummatory phase of action see his *The Philosophy of the Act*, pp. 445–53.

21. The "Dewey and Tufts" *Ethics*, published in 1908, was for decades one of the most influential texts in American philosophy.
22. It may be remarked that in "political theory," as in "ethical theory," a distinction may be made between designative (or "factual") statements about political communities, and the evaluation (the appraisal and prescription) of political communities. Dewey's political (and ethical) thought had both elements.
23. Such as Dewey's *Individualism, Old and New; Liberalism and Social Action; Freedom and Culture;* and *Problems of Men*.
24. For a comparison to Gandhi on this point, see *Gandhi and Pragmatism*, by K. Ramakrishna Rao.
25. For James's statement, see R. B. Perry, *op. cit.*, vol. 1, p. 668.
26. In addition to Dewey's *Art as Experience* and some chapters in his *Experience and Nature*, there is a paper by Mead, "The Nature of Aesthetic Experience" (reprinted with some omissions in *The Philosophy of the Act*, pp. 454–57), chapters 14 and 15 in C. I. Lewis's *An Analysis of Knowledge and Valuation*; a two-volume work, *Art and Freedom*, by Horace M. Kallen, and *Introduction to Beauty* by Van Meter Ames.
27. John Dewey, *Reconstruction in Philosophy*, p. 127.
28. See "The Logical Foundations of Peirce's Aesthetics," by Max O. Hocutt.
29. This position has been developed by the present author in a number of studies. See chapter 5 ("Art, Signs, and Values") of *Signification and Significance*, for a discussion of the general position and for references to other articles. There is an analysis of the term "expressive" in *Signs, Language, and Behavior*, pp. 67–71.
30. William James, *The Varieties of Religious Experience*, p. 35.
31. In addition to the references to Mead in the text, important sources for the pragmatists' views on religion include the following: Peirce, *Collected Papers*, 9.395–556; James, *The Varieties of Religious Experience*; Dewey, *A Common Faith*; Edward Scribner Ames, *The Psychology of Religious Experience, Prayers and Meditations*, and *Religion*; Horace M. Kallen, *Secularism Is the Will of God*. Two of my books are relevant to the relation of religion and values: *Paths of Life: Preface to a World Religion*, and *Varieties of Human Value*.

V

Pragmatic Cosmology

1. *"Cosmology" or "Metaphysics"?*

It would be possible to entitle this chapter "Pragmatic Metaphysics." To do so would indeed be appropriate to Peirce's terminology.[1] Peirce asked what would remain of philosophy if the pragmatic maxim were accepted—a maxim which limited admissible hypotheses to those capable of verification—and his answer was this:

... what will remain of philosophy will be a series of problems capable of investigation by the observational methods of the true sciences. . . . In this regard, pragmaticism is a species of prope-positivism. But what distinguishes it from other species is, first, its retention of a purified philosophy; secondly, its full acceptance of the main body of our instinctive beliefs; and thirdly, its strenuous insistence upon the truth of scholastic realism. . . . So, instead of merely jeering at metaphysics, like other prope-positivists, whether by long drawn-out parodies or otherwise, the pragmaticist extracts from it a precious essence, which will serve to give life and light to cosmology and physics. At the same time, the moral applications of the doctrine are positive and potent; and there are many other uses of it not easily classed. (5.423)

Here Peirce thinks of pragmatism ("pragmaticism") as preserving a "precious essence" from metaphysics, one that will serve "cosmology and physics." This residue will be the traditional metaphysics only insofar as it can be made to rest on observation—hence it will become a "scientific metaphysics." In this sense metaphysics is for Peirce one part of philosophy—the doctrine of the real, the other parts being phenomenology (the study of that which appears) and the normative sciences (aesthetics, ethics, and logic). Some features of Peirce's own metaphysics will soon be considered.

Nevertheless, as a chapter title for this book, "pragmatic cosmology" seems preferable to "pragmatic metaphysics." Peirce himself often made scathing remarks about the traditional metaphysics. Dewey, who had used the term (as in his *Experience and Nature*), came to think it confusing if the term was applied to his views. Mead in general used the term disparagingly. For most of philosophical history "metaphysics" has been opposed to the observational sciences, and for many contemporary writers this is still true.[2] Hence for reasons both within and external to the pragmatic movement, it does not seem desirable to speak of "pragmatic metaphysics" in the present discussion. Therefore, the term "cosmology" has been employed, though that term too has its drawbacks (such as the fact that for Peirce cosmology was only a part of metaphysics). At any rate, the concern here is with the pragmatists' views about the "world" or the "universe" or the "cosmos," including man's place in it.

Such a cosmology must be, for the pragmatist, based on experience. It must in principle utilize, and be consonant with, the results of the special sciences; it can differ from the sciences only in terms of generality. It must therefore be formed and tested in the light of the entire range of experience.[3] But in saying this we encounter again a basic problem: what is the pragmatist's conception of experience?

2. *Experience as Content*

In chapter II we discussed at some length the pragmatist's notion of experience in its relation to inquiry and knowledge. Here we will consider experience with respect to cosmology.

There is in the pragmatic movement a tension with respect to this problem inherent in its acceptance on the one hand of the heritage of British philosophic empiricism, and on the other hand of the doctrine of evolutionary biology. For the tradition of British empiricism "experience" was a subject-matter whose contents included such items as sensations, impressions, images, ideas, and thoughts; this domain as a whole was characterized by such terms as "individual," "private," "subjective," "mental," "conscious." Hence the historical problem of the relation of experience to the total world.

Of the pragmatists James was nearest to the British empiricists. One of his main differences from that tradition was his recognition of a much wider range of the contents of experience—as including relations as well as the particulars which are related, and continuities as well as discontinuities. This more richly conceived experience was to be the subject-matter for philosophy. It was in this spirit that he formulated his doctrine of *radical empiricism*. Part of the doctrine was the methodological postulate that "the only things that shall be debatable among philosophers shall be things definable in terms drawn from experience."[4]

Closely connected with this methodological postulate was James's cosmological position, namely, that reality (the "cosmos") itself was to be conceived in experiential terms—this part of the doctrine of radical empiricism he called the "philosophy of pure experience."[5] In considering this conception it is important to note, however, another important deviation of James from the traditional British conception of experience. Experience was no longer conceived as a private mental domain, or even as an awareness or consciousness of certain contents, but "experience" was simply taken as a name for the contents themselves.[6] These contents could enter into relation with a given individual and this gave "knowledge by acquaintance"; and some of these same contents, as objects of acquaintance, could become indications of other contents (leading to them, preparing the individual for them, "substituting" for them) and in this capacity, they gave "knowledge about" these other contents. The cosmos as a whole became simply the totality of "pure experience."

Now this is historically a novel line of thought, and perhaps shows James at his speculative boldest. It is empiricism freed from subjectivistic and mentalistic encumbrances and made into a cosmology. Historically this view opened the way to the philosophy of American new realism, and also to a functional theory of consciousness.

But paradoxically, equating nature (or reality or the cosmos) with experience deprived the term "experience" of any distinctive meaning,[7] at least in the "hard-core" sense of the pragmatic maxim. If everything in and of itself is an "experience" then the term "experience" has lost its "intellectual" or "cognitive" purport (however appealing this usage may be on other grounds). To say that X is an item of experience is no longer to say anything whatsoever about it. It is significant that James himself regarded his radical empiricism (in its cosmological form) and pragmatism as independent doctrines, holding that it was not necessary for a pragmatist to embrace radical empiricism.[8]

3. *Experience as Interactional*

The conception of experience as a particular kind of subjective content, so characteristic of postmedieval Western philosophy, is necessarily challenged if one accepts—as the pragmatists did—the doctrine of biological evolution. For this doctrine makes no sense unless there is a world in which organisms evolve and with portions of which they interact. The term "experience" might then plausibly refer to some kind of relation between organisms and the wider world of nature of which they are a part. "Experience" signifies a special kind of interaction rather than a special kind of content. "Experience" becomes an occurrence within the cosmos.[9] In such a view, experience would not be content different in kind from the rest of the cosmos. Nor would the cosmos become "a world of pure experience."

The view thus sketched is clearly Dewey's position as formulated in the second edition (1929), p. 49, of his *Experience and Nature*:

Experience is *of* as well as *in* nature. It is not experience which is experienced, but nature—stones, plants, animals, diseases, health, temperature, electricity, and so on. Things interacting in certain ways *are* experience; they are what is experienced. Linked in certain other ways with another natural object—the human organism—they are *how* things are experienced as well.

Note in this formulation that experience is equated with "things interacting in certain ways." Dewey does not here specify these "ways." He merely says that experience "occurs only under highly specialized conditions, such as are found in a highly organized creature which in turn requires a specialized environment. There is no evidence that experience occurs everywhere and everywhen" (p. 3a). There are problems as to how to specify these conditions, and certain schools of philosophy (such as the phenomenologists and certain dualists) do not think these conditions can be specified in terms of Dewey's "naturalism." That problem, however, is not our concern here.

It is important to remember that with respect to experience and its relation to nature, the cosmology of all the pragmatists (in spite of certain other differences) is from the beginning non-Cartesian. And this in two senses: experience is not a "mental" realm different in kind from the rest of the cosmos, and experience is not something inherently "private" or "personal" (at least some things can be experienced by more than one experiencer). Thus all four pragmatists accept the notion of "social" or "common" experience. There are, to be sure, "private experiences," but these can be distinguished only by contrast to common experiences.

The pragmatist notion of experience, in its divergence

from the Cartesian and British empiricist "mentalistic" conceptions, is in many ways similar to Aristotle's conception of experience, but the pragmatist retains a place for, and delineates the importance of, certain features of the private and subjective aspects of experience which in European philosophy had come to be overemphasized.[10]

Experience, then, for Peirce, Mead, and Dewey is a part of the cosmos, an occurrence within the cosmos, and since cosmology in this philosophy must be based on observation, the cosmos as experienced is the base upon which generalized cosmological categories and theories must be built and tested. "Experience," writes Dewey, "is not a verb that shuts man off from nature; it is a means of penetrating continually further into the heart of nature."[11]

4. *Peirce's Three Categories*

Philosophy for Peirce is an observational science, differing from the special sciences in that "it contents itself with observations such as come within the range of every man's normal experience" (1.241). This observation is of two sorts: phenomenological observation in a general sense (phenomenology deals with "all that in any sense appears") and observation of signs. Peirce thinks that phenomenological observation discloses (at least) three types of phenomena: qualities, brute reactions of something with something else, and habitual reactions. Peirce employs various sets of terms for these three types of phenomena: "quality, reaction, and mediation" (1.530); "quality," "fact," and "law"; "possibility," "existence," and "habit." His most general title is "Firstness," "Secondness," and "Thirdness." Firstness is variously characterized in terms of quality, possibility, chance, spontaneity; Secondness in terms of reaction, fact, existence; Thirdness in terms of mediation, law, habit, universality, generality, continuity. These are the three Peircean categories. Peirce says of them: "Perhaps it is not right to call these categories conceptions; they are so intangible that they are rather tones or tints upon conceptions" (1.353).

Peirce believed that this phenomenologically based triadic analysis was supported by the study of signs, he found only three main kinds of signs (icon, index, and symbol), and only three main kinds of propositions,[12] depending on the number of subjects the predicates required for a complete proposition to be formed (these he called monadic, dyadic, and triadic propositions—illustrated by "x is red," "x hits y," "x gives y to z"). These three kinds of signs and propositions were regarded by Peirce as instances of the three general categories, and since he thought that analysis disclosed only three kinds of signs and three kinds of propositional forms, he took this as strong evidence that there were only three categories of the real.

It may be noted, however, that at times Peirce does not deny that there may be other conceptions perhaps as general as the three categories he considered as basic (1.526). Also it may be noted that while the categories must in Peirce's philosophy be in some sense "experienced" this does not mean that they are objects of "perception," for "the concept of *experience* is broader than that of *perception*" (1.336). Finally, with regard to the difficulty in applying Peirce's pragmatic maxim to the analysis of the meaning of the categories themselves, it must be remembered that Peirce does not strictly limit meaning to the criterion expressed in the early formulations of the pragmatic maxim.

Peirce's terminology and analysis with respect to the categories do not play a prominent part in the writings of any other pragmatist. Nevertheless, I think that the pragmatists here under consideration, whatever their terminology, ascribe to the cosmos the characteristics signified in the three Peircean categories. Since Peirce meant by a "nominalist" anyone who denied the reality of Thirdness, it follows that none of these pragmatists were nominalists in Peirce's sense.

It is not difficult to find a recognition of the three Peircean categories in Dewey's writings. We will restrict our attention to his *Experience and Nature*.[13] Here Dewey speaks of "the mixture of universality, singularity, and chance" in nature (p. 48). His opposition to nominalism is explicit (pp. 84–85): he writes that "a continuous way of organized action is not a particular" (p. 196); and that "every meaning is generic or universal" (p. 187). In Dewey the notion of quality plays an important part: "all existences . . . have qualities of their own" (p. 108); there is "something unpredictable, spontaneous, unformulable, and ineffable . . . in any terminal object" (p. 117); and Dewey himself wrote a sympathetic article entitled "Peirce's Theory of Quality." As for Secondness, Dewey's very conception of experience is one of "doings and sufferings" (or "undergoings") (p. 358); he expressly holds that "there is no action without reaction" (p. 73), and that "only action, interaction, can change or remake objects" (p. 158). A similar analysis could be given of Mead's writings.

James might seem to be the most likely exception to the view that all three of the Peircean categories are found in all the pragmatists. James certainly does stress Firstness (as possibility, quality, indeterminateness) more than Secondness (as reaction) or Thirdness (as law or generality). "Pure experience," he writes, is "but another name for feeling or sensation" (*Essays in Radical Empiricism*, p. 94): " 'Substance' means that a definite group of sensations will recur" (*Some Problems in Philosophy*, p. 62). Certainly "physical things" in "brute reaction" are not as prominent in James as they are in Peirce or Mead. And yet James's constant stress on pluralism (the view that "the sundry parts of reality *may be externally related*") (*A Pluralistic Universe*, p. 321) does not exclude the possibility of reactions among these parts (which are certainly existents)—and to that extent is compatible with Secondness. Thirdness is clearly recognized by James. He insists upon the continuities within experience as much as upon the discontinuities, and this view, which he calls "synechistic pluralism," he ascribes to Peirce (and to Bergson) as well as to himself.[14]

5. *Peirce's Cosmology: Evolutionary Idealism*

Pragmatic cosmology is consistently evolutionary: the cosmos is envisaged throughout the movement as a developmental process. But within this common agreement there is a sharp difference between the evolutionary idealism of Peirce and the evolutionary naturalism of Dewey and Mead. Peirce called his cosmology "a Schelling-fashioned idealism which holds matter to be mere specialized and partially deadened mind"[15] (6.102); Mead in contrast wrote: "I have wished to present mind as an evolution in nature, in which culminates that sociality which is the principle and the form of emergence" (*The Philosophy of the Present*, p. 85). In one case the evolution of the cosmos is intrinsically mental; in the second case mind is one emergent within evolving nature. The issues are complicated, but some light can be thrown upon the cause of these cosmological differences.

In a famous passage Peirce presents his picture of cosmological development in these words:

Such are the materials out of which chiefly a philosophical theory ought to be built, in order to represent the state of knowledge to which the nineteenth century has brought us. Without going into other important questions of philosophical architectonic, we can readily foresee what sort of a metaphysics would appropriately be constructed from these conceptions. Like some of the most ancient and some of the most recent speculations it would be a Cosmogenic Philosophy. It would suppose that in the beginning—infinitely remote—there was a chaos of unpersonalized feeling, which being without connection or regularity would properly be without existence. This feeling, sporting here and there in pure arbitrariness, would have started the germ of a generalizing tendency. Its other sportings would be evanescent, but this would have a growing virtue. Thus, the tendency to habit would be started; and from this, with the other principles of evolution, all the regularities of the universe would be evolved. At any time, however, an element of pure chance survives and will remain until the world becomes an absolutely perfect, rational, and symmetrical system, in which mind is at last crystallized in the infinitely distant future. (6.33)

Though Peirce does not in this passage refer to his categories, it is not difficult to interpret the view there expressed in those terms. The "chaos of unpersonalized feeling" in the "infinitely remote" beginning is Firstness (quality, feeling, possibility, spontaneity). The "habit" or "generalizing tendency" is Thirdness (continuity, generality, habit, thought, mind). And this Thirdness in its development gradually brings into existence (Secondness) a world which is "crystallized" mind and which in "the infinitely distant future" will be "absolutely perfect, rational, and symmetrical." Thus Thirdness (mind) transforms Firstness (possibility) into determinate forms of Secondness (existence). Since "matter" is essentially Secondness given a determinate character by mind, it can be regarded as "specialized and partially deadened mind." The whole process in which mind "crystallizes" itself into a determinate world is the cosmological process of "concrete reasonableness." Such is Peirce's "objective idealism."

No other pragmatist has held an idealistic metaphysics of this sort. There are critics who have argued that this Peircean ("Platonic," "Schellingean," "Hegelian") metaphysics not only antedates Peirce's pragmatism but is incompatible with it. Certainly if one stresses the "hard-core" version of the pragmatic maxim one can show the difficulties in translating this idealistic cosmology into a set of statements that if such and such actions are performed, such and such observable consequences will be obtained. But we have previously seen that Peirce himself did not regard this hard-core interpretation as a complete account of theoretically meaningful symbols. And Peirce certainly thought of his pragmatism as lending support to his hypothesized idealistic cosmology ("hypothesized" since Peirce repudiated all claims of philosophers to dogmatic finality) rather than being in opposition to it.

Peirce constantly emphasized the way in which an existing state of affairs is changed by human thought. Thus a person opens a closed window to change the stuffy air in a room. Here a possibility (a closed window being opened) is envisaged, and the thought of obtaining fresh air under these circumstances leads to the actual opening of the window; thought (Thirdness) has actualized (Secondness) a possibility (Firstness).[16] This observed phenomenon "read large" becomes the prototype of Peirce's cosmology. But what is the warrant for this cosmic extension of a characteristic form of human conduct? Peirce would reply: "the principle, or maxim, of continuity, that we ought to assume things to be continuous as far as we can . . ." (6.277). The cosmos as a whole is to be envisaged as continuous with the cosmos as observed— "as far as we can." The process of human thought is then a phase of cosmic thought. Man can trust his reasoning as in the long run conforming to the nature of things. He can gain support for accepting reasonableness as his ideal of life, for concrete reasonableness is cosmological reality.

The issue of the relation of Peirce's pragmatism to his cosmological views can be sharpened if we recall that the interpretant of a symbol, earlier called a "thought," was described in his later analysis in terms of the generality of a "habit." Peirce was also much impressed with the fact that the interpretant of a symbol tended in turn to become itself a symbol with its own interpretant—an instance of continuity. Finally, the reality of a symbol, involving the generality of a habit, consisted in a law rather than a set of individual reactions. Peirce is impressed with the close relation of the concepts of symbol, thought, habit, law, generality, and continuity, indeed so impressed that they

are used almost interchangeably, and are all brought together to form the category of Thirdness. Call Thirdness
by the name of mind and regard it as directing the actuali-
zation of possibility, and the result is Peirce's objective
idealism.

The identification of mind and Thirdness,[17] however,
rests, as we have seen, upon Peirce's tendency to equate
thought, symbol, habit, and law, as a consequence of his
extreme reliance upon continuity. But if discontinuity were
to be taken as seriously as continuity,[10] it would be possible
not to equate, say, "thought" with "habit" or "law"—and
thus to admit Thirdness as a categorical feature of the
cosmos without embracing a metaphysics of objective
idealism. "Mind" might then "emerge" under certain natural conditions, rather than being the "fountain of existence." Such an evolutionary naturalism is prefigured in
James and given a major development in Mead.

6. James's Denial of Consciousness as an Entity

In *The Principles of Psychology*, James, with the aim of
advancing psychology as an empirical science, deliberately
avoided certain fundamental issues which concerned him
as a philosopher. In that volume he simply postulated or
assumed without discussion that there was a realm of mind
("thoughts," "feelings") and a realm of extramental objects, and that minds know such extramental objects. This
was a "methodological dualism" in which James accepted
for the purpose of psychology the then common view of
the existence of certain intrinsically psychical or mental
realities.

We have already noticed, in the discussion of the pragmatist's conception of experience, that James as a philosopher moved beyond this dualistic position tentatively assumed in *The Principles of Psychology*. He no longer thought of experienced contents as being in their very nature psychical or mental. A brown color, for instance, could be regarded as "physical" if considered in relation to the desk of which it was the color, and as "mental" if considered in relation to the biography of the person seeing the brown desk. The brown color as such would be neither mental nor physical.

A second decisive step was taken when James argued that the thought about something (consciousness in the sense of "conscious of") was also not a special kind of "entity" or "stuff" but a functional affair of one item in experience serving as a substitute for another by directing conduct with respect to that for which it was a substitute. James did not himself make much use of semiotical terminology, but it is not unfair to say that on this analysis, consciousness (in the sense of consciousness of something) is the functioning of signs, and anything apprehended may so function as a sign. "Mind" in this sense is a sign-process. This aspect of James's thinking, prefigured in the chapter on conception[19] in *The Principles of Psychology*, is explicitly formulated in his 1904 article "Does 'Consciousness' Exist?"[20]

James's answer to this rhetorical question was a decisive "No!" Consciousness (as thought) is not some kind of pure awareness: *"Thoughts in the concrete are made of the same stuff things are"* (p. 37). The distinction of thought and thing, of knower and known, is a functional distinction which arises in experience. If we call what is present in experience a "percept," then a concept is a percept which is a substitute for other percepts, which directs behavior to them, which "means" them. When this functional situation obtains we say (in this analysis) that we have something "in mind." "Consciousness connotes a kind of external relation, and does not denote a special stuff or way of being" (p. 35).

Peirce wrote to James about the article "Does 'Consciousness' Exist?" the same month in which it appeared (see 8.279–85). It is clear that he did not understand what James was driving at: he wrote, "Your paper floors me at the very opening . . . it is barred to me until I can find out what it is that you are opposing" (8.279). James replied in a letter that he was opposing the view that "consciousness" meant "a *constituent principle* of all experience, as contrasted with a certain *function or relation* between particular parts of experience" (quoted by the editor in note 31 to 8.285). In his relational analysis of "consciousness" and in his functional analysis of "consciousness of" James was expressing a view directly contrary to Peirce's own view that mentality is a categorical feature of reality. James's position would not lead to the cosmology of objective idealism. It is humanly comprehensible why Peirce did not understand what James was getting at in the relational and functional turn of his analysis.

This important difference should not obscure the fact that James and Peirce agree in regarding mind (as "thought of" or "consciousness of") as a sign or symbol process. The difference between them lies in the cosmological extension (or range) given to sign processes.

7. Mead: Language, Mind, and Self

In the chapter on pragmatic semiotic it was pointed out that Mead's greatest contribution to the theory of signs was his behavioral analysis of the linguistic symbol. For Mead human language was an elaboration of animal gestural communication in which the signs had gained a common signification (by having a common behavioral interpretant) to the producer and receiver of the signs alike. On his analysis the uttered sound held a place of central importance because it was heard by the one who uttered the sign as well as by others; hence spoken language was regarded as the prototype of all other forms of language. Language presupposed a social process for its appearance, but having appeared, it in turn made possible complex human society and the human mind and self. Thus starting from a naturalistically conceived biosocial process, Mead sought to account for the appearance of the higher forms of human society and of the human person.

Mead identified mind with the functioning of language symbols. So conceived, mind is not originally an inner psychic world, nor even the brain inside an organism, but a mode of behavior in which individuals interact with other individuals and the surrounding world through the mediation of language symbols.[21] The social linguistic process is however "internalized"[22] in the sense that one may talk to oneself silently or "out loud," and whether alone or in the presence of others. Thinking is for Mead essentially the internalized process of linguistic symbols; it is reflective thought when directed to the solution of problems encountered in behavior. Hypotheses so engendered may be confirmed when acted upon overtly, but they may not be—in which case we are likely to say that they were just "subjective," just "in the mind." But even when internalized, and even when "subjective" in this sense, language symbols are still processes in nature, for the organism is part of nature.

Mead's position also legitimatizes certain usages of the term "private." For a person can to some extent observe himself, and observe features of himself and his behavior (including his sign behavior) which cannot be directly observed by others. Privacy is here a matter of inaccessibility for observation by other persons. But such privacy is not a matter of access to something intrinsically "mental." Nor does such privacy even coincide with what is "inside" the boundary of the organism, for it is possible that something may be observed in the "outer world" that cannot in fact be observed by anyone else—such as the last flower of a given species if observed by an isolated botanist.

Mead is thus able even in his behavioral approach to find signification in such terms as "subjective" and "private"[23]—and this without even a shadow of the Cartesian dualism of the mental and the physical entering into his analysis.

What is the self that on Mead's analysis can discourse with itself?[24] Mead regards the essential characteristic of selfhood to be self-consciousness, in the sense of the capacity to be conscious of oneself as an object. He finds the means of such self-consciousness in language. Because of the social character of language symbols, one calls out in himself the attitudes one's own linguistic symbols call out in others. Hence in symbols referring to one's own minded-organism one responds to oneself as others respond, and hence becomes an object to oneself—becomes conscious of oneself, becomes a self. The self is thus the minded-organism becoming conscious of itself. In this sense of the term Mead believed that animals other than man were not selves, since they lacked the linguistic mechanisms which in his opinion made self-consciousness possible.

Such in brief outline are the central points of Mead's views on the human mind as a symbol process at the linguistic level, and on the human self as a minded-organism capable of bringing itself within the scope of its own symbolic references. What is the cosmological anchorage and import of man so conceived?

8. *Mead's Cosmology of Objective Relativism*

For Mead, in accordance with the combined empirical and biological facets of pragmatism, experience involves a dynamic interaction of an active organism and those features of the environing world to which it is sensitive. In this interactive process, both the organism as experiencing and the world as experienced are changed. Mead regards such a dynamic relation as an instance of a perspective. Thus in an extended sense of the term "social," Mead says that a perspective is social: the nature of something in the perspective is determined (at least in part) by the nature of the other members of the perspective.[25] But what this something is in one perspective will in turn influence what it is when it enters other perspectives—and this is the second sense of the term social. We may thus distinguish two senses of this extended use of the term social:[26] one refers to the mutual influence upon each other of components within a perspective (or system), and the other refers to the influence of what something is in one perspective (or system) upon what it is in other perspectives (or systems). These might be called intraperspectival (or intrasystemic) sociality and interperspectival (or intersystemic) sociality—though Mead himself does not use these terms. The two senses of "social" when combined constitute what Mead calls the "principle of sociality."[27] The new or novel properties which accrue to something when it enters a new perspective (or system) Mead calls "emergent" properties.

At the human level this principle of sociality may be illustrated by the case of a boy raised in a small community who enters a university. Certain features of his personality resulted from his contact with others in the small community—he is a "small-town boy." These features of his personality influence his reactions within the university community, but new features of his personality emerge because of his interactions with others in the university. And this process will continue with every further social situation into which he enters. And of course what has been said holds as well for every other person with whom the boy interacts in the small town and in the university.

The individual is partly what he is because of the perspectives (or systems) of which he was and is a member. He has no nature as a person outside of all such perspectives (or systems), and yet his nature cannot be exhaustively stated in terms of what he is in any one perspective, nor, indeed, can it be stated in terms of any specific set of such perspectives (since new features of his personality would emerge if he entered into new perspectival situations).

Now the cosmological question is whether this type of analysis can be extended to all features of the cosmos. It was clearly Mead's conviction that it can be so extended. "There is no aspect of the universe that is not a perspective" (*Philosophy of the Act*, p. 495).[28] He distinguished three main levels of organization of perspectives—the inorganic, the organic, the mental.[29] He suggested in various places how the objects of each level are social in the sense that each is what it is because of its relations to the other members of each and all of the perspectives in which it enters. At each level the perspectives are organized through the fact that the members of one perspective always occur in other perspectives as well. But the three levels are themselves organized in relation to each other by the same principle of sociality. Thus life is an emergent under certain conditions from the inorganic level, and the human (or mental) level is in turn an emergent from the organic level under certain conditions. This whole complex of perspectives, organized by the principle of sociality, constitutes the cosmos.

This is not the occasion to attempt to delineate in detail, nor to defend, this emergent evolutionary cosmology. But several of its distinctive features may be noted. In the first place, on this view the cosmos is (as it was for James) "one" in some respects and "many" in other respects. It has unity in the sense that no component perspective is isolated, i.e., without some of its members being also in other perspectives; hence the cosmos is "one" as an organized system of perspectives. But it is not "one" in the sense that it is a single all-inclusive perspective. Each thing is in perspectival relation to *some* other things, but not to *all* other things (or put in another way, not all perspectives have all members in common). Hence plurality is as basic as unity. Mead's thought, like James's, has place for both discontinuities and continuities.

In the second place, the position is that of an evolutionary naturalism rather than (as with Peirce) an evolutionary idealism. For Mead regards mind as an emergent, and hence as only one level of the organization of perspectives. This does not mean that Mead has no place for Peircean Thirdness—indeed the principle of sociality, basic to the whole cosmology, is itself a form of Thirdness: what x will be in perspectival relation to y depends in part upon what x is in perspectival relation to z. But whereas Peirce tends to equate mind with Thirdness, Mead's view in effect treats mind as only an emergent form of Thirdness and not as identical with it. It follows that there is nothing in Mead corresponding to Peirce's image of the cosmos as a process of "concrete reasonableness" in which Thirdness (as Mind) constructs out of pure Firstness (as possibility) a world of determinate and rationalized Secondness (as existence or actuality). All of the Peircean categories find a place in Mead's cosmos; but in Mead's cosmological framework each of the categories must involve the others. Hence there could be no possibilities without actualities and no actualities without the Thirdness involved in the principles of sociality (thus emergents are possibilities of actualities, and actualities are what they are only through their participation in a number of perspectival relations to other actualities). In Mead (and

likewise in Dewey), the Peircean categories remain categorical features of reality, but Peirce's evolutionary idealism has become an evolutionary naturalism.

Since on such a cosmology the properties of anything
are its properties in virtue of its perspectival (or systemic)
relations to other objects, properties may be said to be
"objectively relative," and a cosmology which generalizes
this principle may be called a cosmology of objective relativism.[30] In the next section this notion will be developed
at greater length, and the question raised whether pragmatic cosmology as a whole is an evolutionary objective
relativism.

9.   Overview of Pragmatic Cosmology
("Metaphysics")

Metaphysics for Peirce, as a general theory of reality,
is to be based on the observational data of phenomenology
and logic, and is to be checked by a consideration of the
results of the special sciences. Metaphysics so conceived
is an observational science and differs only in degree of
generality from the special sciences—a conception that
differs from certain "speculative" or "rationalistic" views
of metaphysics which distinguished it sharply in method
and in the validity of its conclusions from the observational
sciences. Pragmatists other than Peirce seldom used the
term "metaphysics" or used it disparagingly; hence we
have used the term "cosmology" in this chapter.

The features of the pragmatic cosmology which were
singled out as characteristic were the non-Cartesian con-

ception of experience; the categories of Firstness, Secondness, and Thirdness; the sign (or "semiosical") theory of
mind; and evolutionary objective relativism. On the first
three of these topics there seems to me to be substantial
agreement among the four pragmatists.

Experience is nowhere regarded as a purely private and
intrinsically mental domain set off in sharp distinction
from the rest of the cosmos. Throughout its development
pragmatism has been in opposition to this type of dualism.
In contrast, the domain of experience has been regarded as
part of and continuous with the rest of the cosmos. The
main direction of emphasis was to regard experience as
involving the interaction of the organism and the rest of
the world—essentially a return to an Aristotelian (and
"everyday language") conception. At the same time there
was a recognition of certain private or subjective aspects
of experience, and in this respect the pragmatic treatment
of experience attempted to do justice to prominent features
of the Cartesian-inspired modern tradition.

Though none of the other pragmatists made use of
Peirce's terminology of Firstness, Secondness, and Thirdness, all of them recognized these categorical features of
reality ("possibility," "actuality," "generality") in some
form or other.

All of the major pragmatists conceived of mind in terms
of the operation of signs. There were, however, major
differences of emphasis upon the range and cosmological
importance of mind so conceived—as in the difference between Peirce's evolutionary idealism and Mead's evolutionary naturalism.

On the fourth major characteristic—evolutionary objective relativism—there is a legitimate question as to whether

the objective relativism aspect (though not the evolutionary aspect) can rightly be regarded as applying to pragmatic cosmology as a whole.

It must be admitted at once that no other pragmatist has developed explicitly and in a generalized form the doctrine here ascribed to Mead. But there are many examples and specific analyses in the other pragmatists which seem to me to embody the germ of this doctrine. Thus Peirce writes:

. . . everything which is present to us is a phenomenal manifestation of ourselves. This does not prevent it being a phenomenon of something without us, just as a rainbow is at once a manifestation both of the sun and of the rain (5.283).[31]

Even more relevant in this statement:

And the notion of being such as other things make us, is such a prominent part of our life that we conceive other things also to exist by virtue of their reactions against each other. (1.324)

James, amplifying his statement that "*nothing* real escapes from having an environment" (*A Pluralistic Universe*, p. 319), remarks:

Our "multiverse" still makes a universe, for every part, though it may not be in actual or immediate connexion, is nevertheless in some possible or mediated connexion, with every part however remote, through the fact that each part hangs together with its very next neighbor in inextricable interfusion. (*ibid.*, p. 325)

Dewey, whose position was called an "objective relativism" by Arthur E. Murphy, held that "anything changes according to the interacting field it enters" (*Experience and Nature*, p. 285).[32]

Mead does not apply the exact phrase "objective relativism" to his position, but there are many places where he uses both "objective" and "relation" in the same sentence:

> Just as an object at a distance has a perspective value which is dependent on the relation of the eye to which the lines of light converge . . . so the so-called sensuous quality of the object seen at a distance emerges as the result of its relation to the organism that is sensitive to the object, and this character is as objective as is perspectivity, i.e., belongs to the object, but to the object at a distance. (*The Philosophy of the Act*, p. 283)[33]

An objective relativist cosmology is in a sense a generalization of what is involved in the pragmatic interpretation of experience. In the relation between organisms and world which constitutes experience, both the world and the organism attain characteristics which otherwise they would not have. Generalize this latter fact about the experience relation, but remove the demand that the special conditions of being a sense-equipped biological organism always obtain, and the result is an objective relativist cosmology. It seems to me that the pragmatic cosmology—in addition to being in general a process or temporalistic cosmology—has in its treatment of experience as perspectival (or transactional) the germ of objective relativism which attains its fullest development in Mead.

Such an objective relativism is congruent with many other features of pragmatic thought, such as the treatment of value in relation to the consummatory phase of the act, and the approach to semiotic in which signs signify only through the mediation of an act of the interpreter.

For these reasons objective relativism seems an appropriate designation for the most distinctive aspect of pragmatic cosmology.

NOTES

1. Ontology, cosmology, and religion are for Peirce the subdivisions of metaphysics (1.192).
2. This is so even for certain pragmatists. Thus for C. I. Lewis metaphysics consisted of analytic sentences, and was without cosmological content (*Mind and the World-Order*, chap. 1). I advocated a somewhat similar view in *Signs, Language, and Behavior*, pp. 175–78, thus distinguishing cosmology and metaphysics.
3. These criteria are compatible with a number of hypotheses about the cosmos, and there are in fact considerable differences among the pragmatists in their cosmologies. Hence no perfectly unified "pragmatic cosmology" can issue from this discussion. The differences in cosmological views is perfectly compatible with substantial agreement as to meaning and method, just as a number of physicists might agree on scientific method and yet differ at a given time in their hypotheses held in accordance with that method—an example would be the contemporary scientific differences concerning the origin of the moon.
4. For James's full formulation of "radical empiricism" see the Preface to *The Meaning of Truth*, pp. xii–xiii. The quotation in the text is from p. xii.
5. *Essays in Radical Empiricism*, edited by Ralph Barton Perry, p. 193. On p. 195 James states that the philosophy of pure experience excludes "the hypothesis of transempirical reality." On p. 193 he states: "*Experience as a whole is self-containing and leans on nothing.*"
6. "There is no *general* stuff of which experience at large is made. There are as many stuffs as there are 'natures' in the things experienced. . . . Experience is only a collective name for all these sensible natures . . ." (*Essays in Radical Empiricism*, pp. 26–27).
7. Peirce noted this in a letter to James: "What you call 'pure experience' is not experience at all . . ." (8.301). Peirce did not, however, deny what James was attempting to refer to, but only that "experience" was the proper name.

8. According to James "there is no logical connexion between pragmatism, as I understand it, and a doctrine which I have recently set forth as 'radical empiricism.' The latter stands on its own feet. One may entirely reject it and still be a pragmatist" (Preface to *Pragmatism*, p. ix).

9. Thus for Mead experiencing is "a natural process on the same level of reality as all other natural processes" (*The Philosophy of the Act*, p. 517. Cf. pp. 405–06, 423).

10. It is Mead who works out in most detail the sense in which certain limited aspects of the experiencing of the world may be said to be private or subjective; some reference to this will be made later. I think it should be noted that while the general points of this section seem to me to be correct, the pragmatists have by no means had an easy time with the notion of experience. The differences in the first chapters of the 1925 and 1929 versions of Dewey's *Experience and Nature* are strong evidence of this. James's attempted excursion into a philosophy of pure experience is another. There are considerable differences in Peirce's many references to experience. Lewis bluntly denies the identification of experience with behavior—an identification to which he thinks other pragmatists tend. "Experience" and "empiricism" can certainly no longer be regarded as unproblematic terms!

11. *Experience and Nature*, 1929 edition, p. iii.

12. Or more accurately, propositional functions or propositional forms.

13. The first edition was 1925; the second edition was 1929; the paging is the same except for parts of chapter 1.

14. *A Pluralistic Universe*, pp. 395ff. James explicitly denies that his position is "nominalistic"—for it combines "logical realism with an otherwise empiricist mode of thought" (*Some Problems of Philosophy*, p. 106). An explicit reference by James to Peirce's categories (including Thirdness) is given in R. B. Perry's *The Thought and Character of William James*, vol. 1, p. 525.

15. W. D. Gallie, in *Peirce and Pragmatism*, has made the insightful comment that Peirce's cosmology, as a "world picture," might be regarded as an iconic sign in Peirce's sense of the term. Peirce himself noted that he had not developed the concept of icon as fully as the concept of symbol. It is true that Peirce used the notion of icon in important ways in his philosophy of mathematics, and in his more embryonic aesthetics. But the concept of icon may have much relevance for the interpretation of Peirce himself. Gallie's suggestion that the notion of icon may be important in understanding cosmologies (including Peirce's) deserves serious consideration.

16. Peirce's example of opening a window is found in 5.431.

17. "Psychical" is a wider category for Peirce than "mind," since it embraces both Firstness and Thirdness, while mind (as thought) is Thirdness. The psychical as feeling generally accompanies the psychical as mind or thought, but it need not do so (5.365–66).

18. On the topic of continuity and discontinuity, the reader would do well to refer back to section 7 of chapter III.

19. Mead held that "James's chapter on the concept is the source of his later pragmatism, and of the pregnant ideas which both Royce and Dewey confess that they owe to him" ("The Philosophies of Royce, James, and Dewey, in their American Setting," p. 223).

20. *Journal of Philosophy*, 1, 1904, pp. 477–91. This article is reprinted in *Essays in Radical Empiricism*; the page references in the text are to this book. In this important article James does not distinguish clearly the relational aspects of his theory (which led to "new realism") from the functional aspects (which led to his pragmatism). On this point see my *Six Theories of Mind*, pp. 286–90.

21. "The mental processes do not . . . lie in words any more than the intelligence of the organism lies in the elements of the central nervous system. Both are part of a process that is going on between organism and environment. The symbols serve their part in this process, and it is that which makes communication so important. Out of language emerges the field of mind. It is absurd to look at the mind simply from the standpoint of the individual human organism; for, although it has its focus there, it is essentially a social phenomenon . . ." (*Mind, Self, and Society*, p. 133).

22. Peirce speaks in passing of "the inner world" as "apparently derived from the outer" (5.493) and of thinking as "dialogic in form" (6.338). I discussed these and other similarities to Mead in an early article, "Peirce, Mead, and Pragmatism."

23. For discussions by Mead of *privacy* and *subjectivity*, consult the index of *The Philosophy of the Act*. See also the references to *imagery*.

24. On the self, see Mead's *Mind, Self, and Society*, especially pp. 135–226. Also his article "The Genesis of the Self and Social Control." James had remarked that man differs from animals in his "self-consciousness or reflective knowledge of himself as a thinker" (*Principles of Psychology*, vol. 2, p. 359), but he gave no explanation of this in terms of language symbols. The same may be said with respect to Peirce's statement: "We become aware of ourself in becoming aware of the not-self" (1.324).

25. See *Philosophy of the Present*, p. 77, where "system" is used instead of "perspective." The relation of these concepts is but one of the many issues to be dealt with by future students of Mead's cosmological thinking. Mead's work as social psychologist has received much attention and acclaim; his cosmological thought is largely untouched as yet, and may be of equal importance. Future students will have to explore carefully the relation of Mead's thought to Whitehead's metaphysics, and to the physical theory of relativity.

I would like to record two points Whitehead made in a conversation with me in October 1933. The first was that he thought his philosophy embodied all the main insights of pragmatism. The second was his belief that the pragmatic movement could be greatly strengthened if it explicitly developed a cosmology. His opinion was that his own cosmology seemed to be the sort of thing that was needed.

Whitehead also remarked that he had just been reading Mead's *Philosophy of the Present*, and held Mead in high regard. Mead's unexpected death from a heart attack in 1931 prevented the development of the cosmology of which *The Philosophy of the Present* is only a fragment. And it prevented him from squaring his accounts with Whitehead's *Process and Reality* which appeared not long before Mead's death. Mead's discussions of Whitehead consider only Whitehead's earlier work. That this work had a decisive influence on Mead's development is clear from his paper "The Objective Reality of Perspectives." This important paper, delivered in 1926 and published in 1927 in the *Proceedings of the Sixth International Congress of Philosophy*, is reprinted in *The Philosophy of the Present* (pp. 161–75) and in A. J. Reck's *Selected Writings of George Herbert Mead* (pp. 306–19).

26. *The Philosophy of the Act*, pp. 609–10.
27. *The Philosophy of the Present*, pp. 51–52, and 76–77. Two of Mead's statements about perspectives are as follows: a) "A perspective is the world in its relationship to the individual and his relationship to the world" (*The Philosophy of the Act*, p. 115); b) "A perspective is the continued relationship of a structure to nature which involves change in its maintenance" (*ibid.*, p. 118).
28. In a discussion with Einstein on this matter, his own opinion was negative: objective relativism holds for the world as known by science, but not for metaphysics.
29. See *The Philosophy of the Act*, pp. 606–07.
30. As far as I know, Arthur E. Murphy was the first to introduce the term "objective relativism" (in his 1927 article, "Objective Relativism in Dewey and Whitehead"). Murphy's original enthusiasm for this conception waned as he followed its employment; see his article "What Happened to Objective Relativism?" in *Reason and the Common Good*. It seems to me that Murphy's disenchantment is partly due to a confusion of epistemological and cosmological considerations. I think the concept of objective relativism, and perhaps even the name, are still of basic importance. Ernest Nagel has suggested "contextual naturalism" as a general label for a wide trend in contemporary philosophy of which pragmatism is a part.
31. Note also the important argument of Peirce that "colors are relative to the sense of sight" and yet are "external" (6.327–28). There is much similarity in Peirce's (5.457) and Mead's (*The Philosophy of the Present*, pp. 73–74) general treatment of "secondary qualities."
32. Dewey's article "The Objectivism-Subjectivism of Modern Phi-

losophy" does not specifically deal with objective relativism, yet is very relevant to the topic. The article is reprinted in *Problems of Men*, pp. 309–21. There are also some passages relevant to the topic in *Experience and Nature*, pp. 259, 265, 272.

33. Compare the statement on p. 330 of *Mind, Self, and Society*: "The objects are colored, odorous, pleasant or painful, hideous or beautiful, in their relationship to the organism." Elsewhere Mead writes: "Pleased palates and irritated or suffering members are there in the same sense as other percepts or objects" ("The Genesis of the Self and Social Control," p. 257).

V I

Pragmatism in the
Present

---

1. *On the Unity of the Pragmatic Movement*

The preceding discussions show that while the philosophy
of the American pragmatists is no closed and monolithic
system, there are large areas of agreement among Peirce,
James, Mead, and Dewey, and these occur in all of the
traditional fields of philosophy. If American pragmatism
is not a "system" in the historical sense, it is more systematic than is generally recognized. It stands revealed
as a cooperative movement almost unique in the history
of philosophic thought. Its members are not a group of
disciples centering on and reflecting a master, but a group
of interacting creative thinkers developing various facets
of a common philosophic enterprise. The total result is
one of the major intellectual achievements of the last hundred years.

The main common themes of this philosophic movement
have been reviewed. It focuses upon man as an active

being intelligently seeking to control his future in the direction of his values. At its foundation is a behavioral theory of signs (semiotic). This semiotic serves as the "organon" of the movement. Upon this basis, and influenced strongly by the method of science, the traditional theory of knowledge (epistemology) takes on the new form of the theory of inquiry. Logic and mathematics are explicated within this semiotically grounded theory of inquiry. Evaluation is seen as a special form of the same general type of inquiry found in science, the problem for inquiry in this special case being what to prize in a situation where prizing has become problematic. This type of value theory (axiology) may perhaps be called the view of axiology as the theory of preferential behavior (though this phrase is not employed by the pragmatists themselves).[1] The greatest differences between the pragmatists occur in their views of cosmology (or "metaphysics"). But even here there is agreement that cosmological inquiry must be guided and tested by observation, and that the experienced world in all its richness must be regarded as part and parcel of whatever total reality is recognized. Further, since all the major pragmatists equate mental processes with sign processes, there is common agreement on what might be called a semiosical (or sign) theory of mind.

These common themes, then, characterize pragmatic philosophy in its technical aspects and give it its distinctive cast: a behavioral semiotic; a semiotically interpreted logic; an epistemology oriented around the study of inquiry; an axiology conceived as the study of preferential behavior (that is, of prizing and appraising); a view of experience as an integral part of the cosmos; and a semiosical theory of mind. These are the major common themes, and a novel harvest they are indeed.

This is not to deny important differences among Peirce, James, Mead, and Dewey—differences in personality, in characteristic problems, and even in proposed solutions. Each is a philosopher in his own right; each may be profitably read without consideration of the others. Indeed, insofar as it is "one" the pragmatic movement is a "one in many." I would only argue that the oneness is as important as the manyness, and that in some respects the manyness is additive to form the oneness. For instance, what Peirce had to say about signs and what Mead had to say is very different indeed, but they do not contradict each other and both contribute greatly to an actionally oriented semiotic. Or as another example, Peirce's extreme stress on the community and James's extreme stress on the individual serve to make richer the reciprocal relation between individuality and sociality brought out forcibly by Mead and Dewey.[2] And if one seeks in pragmatism a framework that covers all the traditional areas of philosophy, one will have to consider the work of all four men as complementary.

In the opening chapter an attempt was made to isolate four factors in the cultural situation in which pragmatism originated and which were accepted as unproblematic by the pragmatists. I think it is now evident from the preceding analyses that these four factors did operate in the way claimed: all of the pragmatists were empiricists; all of them respected science and scientific method; all of them felt the impact of evolutionary biology; all of them worked as humanists within the framework of American democratic ideals.

The decade of the 1930's was a period of special importance for the history of American pragmatic philosophy. By the end of that period all the major work of the founders of the movement was available: the first six volumes of Peirce's *Collected Papers*; four volumes of Mead material; and Dewey's *Art as Experience*, *Theory of Valuation*, *Logic*, *A Common Faith*, and *Freedom and Culture*—all completed within a few remarkably productive years.

But 1939 saw the beginning of World War II. This war signalized a new era in American culture. It was impossible to deal at depth at that troubled time with the rich harvest of Peirce, Mead, and Dewey material which the period of the 1930's had just made available.

Further, American philosophers were confronted during that period by powerful European philosophic movements: logical empiricism, late British analytic philosophy, phenomenology, and existentialism. Much of the philosophic thinking in the United States for the last thirty years has centered on this confrontation. It seemed to some thinkers during that time that pragmatism had become of only historical importance.

The matter, however, has proved not to be so simple. For some American thinkers, though often "in the wings" rather than in the spotlight on the philosophic stage, have in recent years been working over, assimilating, and in some respects developing, the historic body of pragmatist thought.

It also turns out that the four listed European movements in philosophy are related to some phases of pragmatism in largely unsuspected ways. They have to some degree been working in different cultural traditions on

144

similar problems, and often with similar (though differently expressed) results. This is beginning to be realized, and comparisons beginning to be made. The result is that some phases of the thought of Peirce, James, Mead, and Dewey have again come into the center of attention, and are as "contemporary" as anything in present-day philosophy.

2. *Pragmatism in the United States Today*

The main work on pragmatism now going on in the United States is primarily (though not exclusively) that of interpretation and assessment. The major activity is undoubtedly on the Peirce material. Two further volumes were added in 1958 to the *Collected Papers*, with Arthur W. Burks as editor, bringing the total to eight.[3] Microfilms of the Peirce manuscripts at the Harvard University libraries have recently been made available. *The Transactions of the Charles S. Peirce Society* supply an important forum of discussion. A number of books on Peirce have very recently appeared, some of which have been referred to in previous notes to this study.[4] Max H. Fisch is at this time finishing a long-awaited biography of Peirce.

Recognition of the importance of Mead's thought continues to grow. A detailed study of Mead's philosophical social psychology has been made by Tom Clifton Keen.[5] Mead's cosmological ideas, as found in *The Philosophy of the Act* and *The Philosophy of the Present* have not yet had the philosophical attention they deserve. This is an important part of Mead's later thought, placing his philosophy of mind in its cosmological setting. David L. Miller will deal with these matters in the study of Mead on which he is now engaged.

The greatly increased attention given of late to William James is often less concerned with James as pragmatist than with the phenomenological aspects of his *Principles of Psychology*, his *Essays in Radical Empiricism*, and with the existentialist affiliations of his *Varieties of Religious Experience*.[6] Interest in James is not limited, however, to these relations. There are several recent anthologies of his thought as a whole.[7] His emphasis on freedom, individualism, and pluralism has been a consistent theme of James's student and friend, Horace M. Kallen, throughout his long and distinguished career.[8]

The "Dewey Project (Cooperative Research on Dewey Publications)" has begun to publish an edition of Dewey's writings. This project is centered at Southern Illinois University; the editorial board includes, among others, George E. Axtelle, Jo Ann Boydston, S. Morris Eames, Lewis E. Hahn, and William A. Leys.[9] A *Dewey Newsletter* has been issued by this group since 1967. Sidney Hook has consistently and with vigor presented and defended Dewey's mode of thought.[10] The journals, especially the *Journal of Philosophy*, contain many articles on aspects of Dewey's philosophy in recent years. His *Art as Experience* continues to be influential, perhaps more so, for the moment, than his social views. It is to be hoped that George Dykhuizen will publish a biography of Dewey, including and continuing the excellent articles he has published on stages of Dewey's career.

No attempt will be made here to characterize the extensive influence of the major pragmatists upon contemporary American philosophers, or upon European philosophers who have come to reside in the United States. This would constitute a study in itself. Material relevant to this topic can be found in the anthology *Pragmatic Philosophy*, edited by Amelie Rorty; in Andrew J. Reck's *The New American Philosophers*; in Morton G. White's *Toward Reunion in Philosophy*; and in the article by Murray G. Murphey, "Kant's Children: The Cambridge Pragmatists."

The thought of C. I. Lewis is receiving much attention at present. Reference has already been made to the recent volumes of essays, *The Philosophy of C. I. Lewis*, edited by Paul A. Schilpp. Some writings left unpublished at his death in 1964 have appeared under the title *Values and Imperatives*, edited by John F. Lange.

3. *Pragmatism and Current European Philosophy*

Concerning the general relation of pragmatism to certain other movements in contemporary philosophy (logical empiricism, late British analytical philosophy, phenomenology, and existentialism), it is to be noted that these five movements developed independently of each other on the backgrounds of different cultural traditions. And except for some merging of later phenomenology and existentialism this is still largely the case, and the workers in one tradition seldom know what has been done in the other movements. Yet a little reflection shows that these movements have a number of features in common; and the preceding analysis of pragmatism may help to suggest how their admittedly different emphases are legitimate and even ultimately complementary.

All five of these movements are cooperative in character —the products of a number of thinkers and not just footnotes on the work of a single master. They are open ended and not "systems" in any historical sense. They are all liberally empirical in temper and in opposition to traditional analyses of experience and traditional speculative metaphysics, especially of the Cartesian type. And they are all "man-oriented": they all at least start from man as focus—his actions, his experience, his language, his linguistic constructions, his attitudinal orientations. The aspects of man attended to are very different in these movements, for the problems with which they are concerned are very different. This accounts for the frequent hostility between members of different movements, for what is relevant to one problem may be quite irrelevant with respect to another—and so may seem unimportant. Yet since the initial focus is upon man's experience and activity, emphases and results of the various movements should complement and not negate each other.

The preceding analysis of the pragmatic movement suggests one perspective from which this complementarity can be seen. Each of the other four movements mentioned stress in fact one of the problem areas central to the pragmatic movement taken as a whole.

Thus the logical empiricism of the Vienna Circle has in common with pragmatism (and Peirce in particular) the joint stress upon formal logic and an empirical criterion of the scientifically meaningful concept and hypothesis. British analytic philosophy in its Wittgensteinian linguistic form, agrees in a rough and general way with pragmatism in the linkage of meaning and action. With respect to phenomenology, there is an explicit place for phenomenology in Peirce and James, and much of Mead's writing (as in *The Philosophy of the Present*) is phenomenological in character. The existentialists' concern (in very diverse forms) for an attitude or way of life appropriate to modern man is a basic problem for all pragmatists, and especially for James and Dewey. Thus these four movements have each manifested concerns shared by the pragmatists, and insofar as the pragmatic movement forms a whole, then these other movements in contemporary philosophy should also prove to be complementary. All five of them may be regarded as specializations within a sustained attempt of present-day man to understand himself and his activities, and to bring himself into focus in this period of basic transformation within human history.

A serious attempt to look at contemporary philosophy in this way would be a large task. It would require studies of the other philosophic movements such as has been attempted here for pragmatism. Then a comparative study of such results would have to be made to find out what the various movements have in common and where they differ, and thus to find out the extent to which they are in fact complementary. Such a "comparative contemporary philosophy" is obviously beyond the limits of this study.

However, there do exist many suggestions of similarities between philosophers in the different movements.[11] In limited ways the fences are already being broken down, and this can be expected to continue. The multiple forces and resources of contemporary philosophy may then be seen in relation to the planet-wide task of modern man to understand himself and to prepare his future.[12]

4. Pragmatism as an Expression of
American Culture

Our main interest has been in pragmatism as a body of
ideas, and not as a phase of cultural history.[13] But we did
stress at the outset the principle, congenial to pragmatism
itself, that a philosophy does arise out of the problems of
specific persons under specific social conditions. In this
sense a philosophy (as any other system of signs) may
be said to "express" its cultural matrix even if it does not
specifically refer to that matrix. As Dewey has pointed
out, a philosophy may (implicitly or explicitly) look with
favor upon its cultural matrix or may react against the
situation under which it develops. Pragmatic philosophy
is expressive of American culture in both respects: it
supports certain aspects of this culture and is highly critical of certain other aspects. And this is true of all of the
founding pragmatists.

Peirce believed that the political achievement of the
United States was its voluntary unification, and this he
thought might form a model for the further development
of the human community.[14] But Peirce was vitriolic in
condemnation of the "gospel of greed" endangering
America, and to this he opposed the "gospel of love." James
welcomed individualism and pluralism, but he vigorously
opposed the cult of "the bitch-goddess Success" and the
American political imperialism of his time. Mead was
perhaps the most optimistic as to the outcome of the
processes at work in the United States, but he was keenly
aware of the continual social reconstruction which the

extension of the democratic ideal required: throughout his life he was concerned with such issues as the social-settlement, the conscientious objector, industrial education, and the transformation of "impulsive charity to social reconstruction." And while Dewey was distinctly a protagonist of American democracy, his criticism of many features of existing American society was very severe.

However critical in detail, pragmatic philosophy was certainly a positive expression of certain practices in American history, and in general of democracy when this is morally interpreted.

As pioneers moving into a rich undeveloped land, the early Americans had confidence in their ability through intelligent activity to meet the problems they encountered and to build a society appropriate to their aspirations and activities. It is true that they had support for their confidence in themselves and their aspirations in certain political and religious views they brought from Europe. But their main reliance was upon themselves as individuals, and upon the piecemeal way in which they resolved their specific problems. In this stress upon the situation lay their uniqueness, and this they did not derive from their inherited culture. However much their political and religious heritage gave them confidence, it did not clarify or justify their actual practices.

James celebrated the essentially individualistic wellsprings of American practices while Peirce, Mead, and Dewey stressed the need of social commitment for the intelligent and moral direction of such individualism. In this way the pragmatic movement gave philosophic expression to practices and ideals which had not received formulation in the culture imported from Europe. It is in this sense that American pragmatism is the positive philosophical expression of American democracy.

Mead has dealt with this matter in his penetrating paper "The Philosophies of Royce, James, and Dewey, in their American Setting." The following words from the concluding paragraph of this paper delineate the situation lucidly:

I have indicated what seems to me the important characteristic of American life, the freedom, within certain rigid but very wide boundaries, to work out immediate politics and business with no reverential sense of a pre-existing social order within which they must take their place and whose values they must preserve. We refer to this as individualism, perhaps uncouth, but unafraid. In its finest form it was embodied in William James, for it was in him refined by a genuine native culture. Now there is only one way in which such an individualism can be brought under constructive criticism, and that is by bringing the individual to state his ends and purposes in terms of the social means he is using. You cannot get at him with an ethics from above, you *can* reach him by an ethics that is simply the development of the intelligence implicit in his act. I take it that it is such an implicit intelligence that has been responsible for the steady development and social integration that has taken place in the American community, with little leadership and almost entirely without ideas. It is hardly necessary to point out that John Dewey's philosophy, with its insistence upon the statement of the end in terms of the means, is the developed method of that implicit intelligence in the mind of the American community.

These are illuminating words. I trust, however, that this book as a whole has shown that American pragmatism is much more than the voice of its historic occasion.

NOTES

1. My article using this phrase, "Axiology as the Science of Preferential Behavior," is in *Value: A Cooperative Inquiry*, edited by Ray Lepley, pp. 211–22.
2. See *Individualism: Personal Achievement and the Open Society*, by David L. Miller.
3. Vol. 7, *Science and Philosophy*; vol. 8, *Reviews, Correspondence and Bibliography*.
4. See the references in the Notes and Bibliography to books by John T. Fitzgerald, W. D. Gallie, Murray G. Murphey, and Vincent G. Potter. There are also references to some volumes of essays on Peirce.
5. Tom Clifton Keen, "George Herbert Mead's Social Theory of Meaning and Experience" (Ph.D. dissertation, Ohio State University, 1968).
6. See especially *The Radical Empiricism of William James*, by John Wild.
7. *The Writings of William James*, edited by John J. McDermott; *Introduction to William James*, edited by Andrew J. Reck.
8. As in Kallen's books *The Liberal Spirit* and *Cultural Pluralism and the American Idea*. A memorial volume of essays was edited in 1947 by Sidney Hook and Milton R. Konvitz, with the title *Freedom and Experience*.
9. S. Morris Eames of this group has written a number of articles on Dewey. The first two volumes of *The Early Works of John Dewey* were published in 1968 and 1969 by the Southern Illinois University Press.
10. References may be found in the bibliography in the book *Sidney Hook and the Contemporary World*, edited by Paul Kurtz. A recent collection of Hook's own writings is entitled *Quest for Being*.
11. I forbear attempting to give specific references at this point. But a few general items, chosen almost at random, are perhaps worth mentioning: Hans Reichenbach traced similarities between his and the pragmatists' treatment of meaning; I have discussed the relation of Carnap to pragmatism in a number of places; Henry Spiegelberg has discussed the connection of James and Peirce to Husserl; John Wild, James Edie, Rollo May, Aron Gurvitsch, Alfred Schutz, Hans Linschoten, among others, have been concerned with the relation of pragmatism (especially James) to phenomenology and existentialism; H. S. Thayer and K. T. Fann have investigated the possible influence of Peirce on Wittgenstein through Frank Ramsey; attention has been called to a number of similarities between Mead and Merleau-Ponty, and between Mead

and Ryle; Van Meter Ames has compared Mead to Sartre and Husserl on the conception of the self; Eugene Kailin has compared the aesthetics of Sartre and Dewey.

12. Though not written from the focus of pragmatism, Edwin A. Burtt's *In Search of Philosophic Understanding*, is especially pertinent to the whole topic of this section.

13. On the topic of this section a useful source is *Pragmatism and American Culture*, edited by Gail Kennedy; it contains a number of essays by pragmatists and their critics, and a general bibliography. H. S. Thayer's *Meaning and Action* includes a discussion of the topic. Also relevant are Herbert W. Schneider's *A History of American Philosophy*, Morton G. White's *Social Thought in America*, and C. Wright Mills's *Sociology and Pragmatism*. The literature on the topic is very extensive.

14. See the essay "Peirce as an American" by Rulon Wells, in *Perspectives on Peirce*, edited by R. J. Bernstein.

Appendix

1.

John Dewey as
Educator*

In his classic work *Democracy and Education* (first published in 1916), Dewey defined philosophy as "the
general theory of education" (p. 383). Education was conceived by Dewey in a wide way, namely as "that reconstruction or reorganization of experience which adds to
the meaning of experience, and which increases ability
to direct the course of subsequent experience" (pp. 89–
90). Taken in this wide sense Dewey conceived of the
philosopher ultimately as educator. "The task of future
philosophy," he writes, "is to clarify men's ideas as to the
moral and social strifes of their own day. Its aim is to
become so far as is humanly possible an organ for dealing
with these conflicts" (*Reconstruction in Philosophy*, p.
26). Certain it is that Dewey conceived his own life task
in these terms, and the enormous body of his writings is

* These pages are portions of a public lecture entitled "John Dewey
as Educator," given at the University of Chicago on August 8, 1951.

made intelligible if we regard it as a sustained attempt at the education of present-day man.

James H. Tufts used to say that *Democracy and Education* was Dewey's finest book. Such later monumental works as *Experience and Nature*, *Art as Experience*, and *Logic: The Theory of Inquiry* are of course more to the interest of the professional philosopher. But the core doctrine of all these books is to be found in a simpler form in *Democracy and Education*. It seems to me that this book exhibits better than any other work the unity of Dewey's thought and the motive of his life.

Democracy and Education gives in its title two terms of Dewey's conceptual trinity; the Preface makes clear that science is the third member. Here is the significant paragraph from the Preface:

The following pages embody an endeavor to detect and state the ideas implied in a democratic society and to apply these ideas to the enterprise of education. The discussion includes an indication of the constructive aims and methods of public education as seen from this point of view, and a critical estimate of the theories of knowing and moral development which were formulated in earlier social conditions, but which still operate, in societies nominally democratic, to hamper the adequate realization of the democratic ideal. As will appear from the book itself, the philosophy stated in this book connects the growth of democracy with the development of the experimental method in the sciences, evolutionary ideas in the biological sciences, and the industrial reorganization, and is concerned to point out the changes in subject matter and method of education indicated by these developments.

In these words Dewey's commitments are evident: he accepts "the democratic ideal"; he accepts the continuity of man and nature implicit in evolutionary biology; he connects the acceptance of the method of experimental science with the growth of democracy; he accepts an industrialized society but believes it requires reorganization; he looks to education as the main agency for the reconstruction of industrial society in the direction of the democratic ideal. Let us now spell out this system-in-miniature by an elaboration of its central concepts.

The stress upon democracy as an ideal is significant; it means that in Dewey's thought democracy is primarily a *moral* conception. In a paper of 1888, entitled "The Ethics of Democracy," are these words. "Democracy is a social, that is to say, an ethical conception, and upon its ethical significance is based its significance as governmental"; democracy is that "form of society in which every man has a chance . . . to become a person." Dewey never departed from this moral conception of democracy as a person-centered society.

In *Democracy and Education* the same stress appears: "If democracy has a moral and ideal meaning, it is that a social return be demanded from all and that opportunities for development of distinctive capacities be afforded for all" (p. 142). The recognition of the importance of individual differences occurs throughout the book (see pp. 45, 87, 137, 153). His frequent tributes to Plato are qualified with respect to this point:

Plato laid down the fundamental principle of a philosophy of education when he asserted that it was the business of education to discover what each person is good for, and to train him to mastery of that mode of excellence, because such development would also secure the fulfillment of social needs in the most harmonious way. His error was not in his qualitative principle, but in his limited conception of the scope of vocations socially needed; a limitation of vision which reacted to obscure his perception of the infinite variety of capacities found in different individuals. (p. 361)

In his stress upon the individual as the seat and source of value Dewey remained squarely within the main cultural tradition of the West.

It is in Dewey's stress upon science that innovations appear. While Dewey regards science as one of the main causes of the contemporary dislocation of society, he also regards it as the main intellectual instrument for overcoming this dislocation. To be sure, this too is the continuation of a tradition. Francis Bacon pointed in this direction, and David Hume wished to extend the experimental method into moral and social subjects. But Dewey, living in a period when psychology and the social studies have become major enterprises, has stressed more than any other contemporary thinker the role of science both in supplying the knowledge needed about man and in supplying men with a method for dealing with their major problems.

At this point we are at a center of contemporary controversy. The term "science" is not only designatively vague and ambiguous, but it has become loaded with attitudes of approval or condemnation. In 1938, in *Experience and Education*, Dewey wrote:

I am aware that the emphasis I have placed upon scientific method may be misleading, for it may result only in calling up the special technique of laboratory research as that is conducted by specialists. But the meaning of the emphasis placed upon scientific method has little to do with specialized techniques. (p. 111)

In his *Theory of Valuation*, also published in 1938, Dewey has this to say of "the scientific attitude":

On its negative side, it is freedom from control by routine, prejudice, dogma, unexamined tradition, sheer self-interest. Positively, it is the will to inquire, to examine, to discriminate, to draw conclusions only on the basis of evidence after taking pains to gather all available evidence. (p. 31)

In the light of such statements, it is seen that Dewey's primary stress is on science as method or attitude; science as organized knowledge consists of those ideas which have stood the test of this method (*Democracy and Education*, pp. 221–24). Dewey's position, then, is that the "great revolution" in science yet to come lies in the solution of the problems of men.

This does not mean that "science" solves human problems; rather that scientific methods and knowledge can be used by men in solving their problems. Dewey is very specific on this point, as indeed his moral commitment to the democratic ideal would require. The chapter on "Social Inquiry" in his *Logic* illustrates this contention:

The difference between physical and social inquiry does not reside in the presence or absence of an end-in-view, formulated in terms of possible consequences. It consists in the respective *subject-matters* of the purposes. . . . In the case of social inquiry, *associated* activities are directly involved in the operations to be performed; these associated activities enter into the *idea* of any proposed solution. The practical difficulties in the way of securing the agreements in actual association that are necessary for the required activity are great. (p. 502)

I take this to mean, in conformity with the democratic ideal, that in a social inquiry the persons for whom something is a problem must themselves partake in the inquiry, must come to agreement on goals and means, and must themselves test the proposed solution in terms of its effects on their lives. If this is so, then when the acceptance of the scientific method is united with the moral ideal of democracy, science is not a means of manipulating men (as in a totalitarian society) but a means by which men may more satisfactorily solve their own individual and common problems.

With this understanding of Dewey's concepts of democracy and science, we now turn briefly to his third basic concept: education. Dewey recognizes that schools differ with societies. So the question is to find the kind of educational system appropriate to a democratic society. The direction of his answer follows from his basic presuppositions. If a democratic society is one in which all persons, to the extent of their abilities, participate in the decisions and the development of the society, and if the method of scientific inquiry is the most effective form of intelligence which man has found for the solution of his problems, then the task of the democratic school is to produce persons with an experimental habit of mind and with the moral character which can cooperate with other persons in associated action consonant with the democratic ideal. In producing such persons the school becomes the main agency for continually transforming an existing state of democracy in the direction of the ideal democracy. Education so conceived is "a freeing of individual capacity in a progressive growth directed to social aims" (p. 115). Its task is "to keep alive a creative and constructive attitude" (p. 231), to liberate "human intelligence and human sympathy" (p. 269).

Let us now consider some of the critical reactions which Dewey's philosophy of education has provoked. That it has been, and is, influential is not of course in doubt. It has transformed the kindergarten and elementary schools. It has been one source of the general education movement. It has been a basic force in the development of adult education. It has influenced schools of design and schools of art education. But it has likewise, from its inception down to today, had its adversaries.

One line of criticism has centered on certain educational practices in many of the schools which raised above themselves the banner of "progressive education." Many of these criticisms have been legitimate. But no one has been more unsparing in criticism of many schools that have used his name than Dewey himself. Since *Democracy and Education* and *Experience and Education* are filled with admonitions and disavowals of such practices, we can dispense here with a detailed analysis of such controversy.

It is frequently said that Dewey is asking too much of the student in the way of originality. To this Dewey replies as follows:

We have set up the notion of mind at large, of intellectual method that is the same for all. Then we regard individuals as differing in the quantity of mind with which they are charged. . . . But this notion of mind in general is a fiction. . . . What is required is that every individual shall have opportunities to employ his own powers in activities that have meaning. Mind, individual method, originality (these are convertible terms) signify the quality of purposive or directed action. If we act upon this conviction, we shall secure more originality even by the conventional standard than now develops. Imposing an alleged uniform general method upon everybody breeds mediocrity in all but the very exceptional. Thus we stifle the distinctive quality of the many, and save in rare instances (like, say, that of Darwin) infect the rare geniuses with an unwholesome quality. (*Democracy and Education*, pp. 202–03)

Another frequent complaint is that Dewey has over-stressed activity in his suggested educational practices. That he has stressed activity is certainly true. But he himself has criticized certain "progressive schools" on the ground that "over-emphasis upon activity as an end, instead of upon *intelligent* activity, leads to identification of freedom with immediate execution of impulses and desires"—which Dewey rejects (*Experience and Education*, p. 81). Intelligent activity—which Dewey calls for—"is distinguished from aimless activity by the fact that it involves selection of means—analysis—out of the variety of conditions that are present, and their arrangement—synthesis—to reach an intended aim or purpose" (*ibid.*, pp. 105–06). Intelligent activity requires imagination, and imagination, Dewey insists, is "a normal and integral part of human activity" (*Democracy and Education*, p. 277).

A related form of criticism is that Dewey's stress upon science has led to a neglect of the importance of the humanities in education. Whatever may be the case in fact, it does not seem that Dewey's thought entails any such neglect. There is, indeed, a genuine sense in which Dewey's philosophy—like Peirce's and Whitehead's—culminates in the sphere of the aesthetic. His book, *Art as Experience*, is certainly one of the most significant contributions to aesthetics made in this century. And a central theme of this book is the high place given to the aesthetic as the consummatory aspect of experience, as "experience in its integrity" (*Art as Experience*, p. 274). That this stress upon the aesthetic is no late afterthought becomes clear if we reconsider his previously quoted criterion of the educative as that "which adds to the meaning of experience, and which increases ability to direct the course of subsequent experience." To stress only the latter part of this criterion would be unfair to Dewey. For the stress upon increasing the richness of experience, so that it reaches an aesthetic or consummatory form, is basic to Dewey's whole philosophical and educational theory. "We always live at the time we live and not at some other time, and only by extracting at each present time the full meaning of each present experience are we prepared for doing the same thing in the future" (*Experience and Education*, p. 51). The same point is made in *Democracy and Education* (p. 65): "Every energy should be bent to making the present experience as rich and significant as possible. Then as the present merges insensibly into the future, the future is taken care of." And as to the high role of the arts in education, the following passage from *Democracy and Education* merits quotation at length:

This enhancement of the qualities which make any ordinary experience appealing, appropriable—capable of full assimilation—and enjoyable, constitutes the prime function of literature, music, drawing, painting, etc., in education. They are not the exclusive agencies of appreciation in the most general sense of that word; but they are the chief agencies of an intensified, enhanced appreciation. As such, they are not only intrinsically and directly enjoyable, but they serve a purpose beyond themselves. They have the office, in increased degree, of all appreciation in fixing taste, in forming standards for the worth of later experiences. They arouse discontent with conditions which fall below their measure; they create a demand for surroundings coming up to their own level. They reveal a depth and range of meaning in experiences which otherwise might be mediocre and trivial. They supply, that is, organs of vision. Moreover, in their fullness they represent the concentration and consummation of elements of good which are otherwise scattered and incomplete. They select and focus the elements of enjoyable worth which make any experience directly enjoyable. They are not luxuries of education, but emphatic expressions of that which makes any education worth while. (pp. 278-79)

When Dewey's philosophy is taken as a whole, it is seen to be a value-oriented philosophy, dedicated to the enrichment and direction of human experience. His stress upon scientific method, and his acceptance of the industrialized civilization which this method has produced, are not capitulations to science and technology. Dewey was first, last, and foremost a humanist, and his whole life was a sustained attempt to humanize science and industry, to turn them to humane ends. The unchanging background of his thought was an allegiance to the creativity of the person, and to democratic society and the democratic school as the extension of the attitude of morality to all interactions of persons.

Historical events since the time of *Democracy and Education* sobered Dewey's writings but did not change his basic convictions. Part 1 of his 1946 book, *Problems of Men*, has as its title "Democracy and Education." Dewey there admits that "the expectations that were entertained by men of generous outlook [around the beginning of the century] are in fact chiefly notable in that the actual course of events has moved, and with violence, in the opposite direction" (p. 23). He makes clear that the road which he has proposed for modern man is very difficult to follow, that science and technology may be used (and are used) to enslave men rather than liberate them, and that faith in control by creative intelligence has seriously weakened. But Dewey's own belief in the significance of the inter-penetration of democracy, science, and education had not altered.

There is no need to dwell upon the enormous obstacles that stand in the way of extending from its limited field to the larger field of human relations the control of organized intelli-gence, operating through the release of individual powers and capacities. There is the weight of past history on the side of those who are pessimistic about the possibility of achieving this humanly desirable and humanly necessary task. I do not predict that the extension will ever be effectively actualized. But I do claim that the problem of the relation of authority and freedom, of stability and change, if it can be solved, will be solved in this way. The failure of other methods and the desperateness of the present situation will be a spur to some to do their best to make the extension actual. They know that to hold in advance of trial that success is impossible is a way of condemning humanity to that futile and destructive oscillation between authoritative power and unregulated indi-vidual freedom to which we may justly attribute most of the sorrows and defeats of the past. . . . The very desperateness of the situation is, for such as these, but a spur to sustained, courageous effort. (pp. 109–10)

This was written when Dewey was seventy-seven. His faith in the potential intelligence, sympathy, and creativ-ity of man had not changed.

2.

Pragmatism and the
Behavioral Sciences*

John Dewey in 1920, in *Reconstruction in Philosophy*, envisaged "the intellectual task of the twentieth century" as follows. Concerning modern science he then wrote:

Roughly speaking, the seventeenth century stressed its application in astronomy and general cosmology; the eighteenth century in physics and chemistry; the nineteenth century undertook an application in geology and the biological sciences.

But, he continued, now

the new ideas and methods should be made at home in moral and social life. Does it not seem to be the intellectual task of the twentieth century to take this last step? When this step is taken the circle of scientific development will be rounded out and the reconstruction of philosophy be made an accomplished fact.[1]

* This material is part of a much longer paper written in 1964.

This point of view is reiterated in the introduction to the 1948 edition of *Reconstruction in Philosophy*. He there stresses the role of philosophers in the seventeenth, eighteenth, and nineteenth centuries in producing a "climate of opinion" favorable to the furtherance of scientific inquiry in the physical sciences. And he expresses the conviction that philosophers now have "the opportunity and the challenge to do a similar work in forwarding moral inquiry."[2]

It is evident from these quotations that Dewey was thinking of an extension of traditional scientific ideas and methods to the study of man—there is no intimation that the human sciences would need to proceed by unique scientific methods. It is also evident that Dewey expected not merely a descriptive science of man, but that the human sciences would also advance "moral inquiry," and hence have normative relevance. Finally, while it is not made explicit in the quotations given, it is certain that for Dewey the science of man which he had in mind would stress action, conduct, behavior.

Pragmatism helped furnish an appropriate climate of opinion for such developments. As Dewey remarked, "A climate of opinion is more than a matter of opinions; it is a matter of cultural habits that determine intellectual as well as emotional and volitional attitudes."[3] Pragmatism expressed the emotional, volitional, and intellectual attitudes which have been dominant in the development of the behavioral sciences in the United States.

Certain earlier thinkers, especially in continental Europe, had been so much impressed by the role of symbols and values in human life that they made a very sharp separation between "natural" and "cultural" sciences, and between the methods used in these two areas of study. At the back of their views was often a philosophical dualism between mind and body, spirit and nature, understanding and knowledge. Such dualisms did not appear in the pragmatic philosophy, and this is perhaps one of the reasons they have not appeared as basic problems for American psychologists and social scientists.

The pragmatists, however, have never been "reductionists," and there is nothing in their approach which requires a denial of the unique complexity of human action. Rather they have made an attempt to approach the admittedly central role which symbols and values play in human life in behavioral terms. The issues here are certainly complicated. But that behavioral scientists without hesitation now study the symbolic and valuational life of man in behavioral terms is certainly in part due to the climate of opinion developed by the pragmatists, and is even in some part due to the analyses which the pragmatists themselves furnished.

I would like now to introduce some data to show that Peirce, James, Mead, and Dewey have in fact exerted an important influence on American workers in the behavioral sciences. A simple questionnaire was sent to the Fellows of the Center for Advanced Study in the Behavioral Sciences. The years covered were 1954–55 through 1962–63. In addition to social scientists and psychologists the membership of the Center has included some philosophers, mathematicians, statisticians, biologists, lawyers, educationalists, literary critics, and a few others.

Three hundred and thirty-five questionnaires were sent out. Philosophers and Fellows trained outside the United States were not included. Two hundred and ten replies were tabulated. These persons were scientists educated in the United States, and most of them, but not all, would call themselves behavioral scientists. The basic information requested was their main field of work; whether the respondent had been influenced in an *important* way by Peirce, James, Mead, or Dewey; if so, by which one or ones; and whether the respondent's teachers had ever acknowledged an important influence by one or more of the four men. The study was informal, so informal in fact that a few of the Fellows wrote they did not wish to take part in it. However, the main results are of interest and relevant to the purposes of this paper.

An important influence on the respondent, by one or more of the four listed pragmatists, was acknowledged by 52 per cent of the respondents. The number of important influences was reported as follows: Dewey (53), Mead (50), James (36), Peirce (21). The respondents fell into the following groups: psychology (48), anthropology (29), political science (27), economics (27), sociology (26), history (15), linguistics (6). The other 32 respondents were lumped together in a "miscellaneous" group.

In terms of fields of study the magnitude of important influence by one or more of the four pragmatists was as follows: sociology (85 per cent), linguistics (67 per cent), psychology (60 per cent), anthropology (55 per cent), miscellaneous (43 per cent), political science (41 per cent), history (33 per cent), economics (30 per cent). Sociology, anthropology, and psychology are often regarded as the "core" behavioral sciences; it is upon them (and the small group of linguists) that the pragmatic influence has been greatest.

Approximately 52 per cent of the respondents wrote that one or more of their teachers had said that one or more of the four pragmatists under consideration had had an important influence upon them. It is noteworthy that there is a close relation between a respondent being importantly influenced by one or more of the pragmatists and his teacher being also so influenced. Thus in 73 per cent of the cases if the respondent claimed an important influence of the pragmatists on him he reported his teachers had claimed such an influence, and if the respondent disclaimed an important influence on himself he reported that his teachers had disclaimed it. Only in 27 per cent of the cases did respondents and teachers disagree on the presence or absence of an important influence by pragmatist thinkers.

These results indicate that Peirce, James, Mead, and Dewey have had a noticeable influence upon the behavioral scientists themselves. Since many of the behavioral scientists sampled are young productive scholars, the influence in question is not merely historical but continues to the present day.

It is hardly necessary to add that this contention is not in contradiction to the statement of Robert K. Merton, in *The Behavioral Sciences Today*, that the roots of contemporary social and psychological science "first took hold chiefly in Europe, not in the United States."[4] Merton in this connection mentions Weber, Durkheim, Fechner, Pavlov, Galton, Freud, and others. Various other writers in the same book speak in the same vein, and there is indeed little reference to the American pragmatists in the occasional historical remarks which occur in this book.

Psychology and the social sciences did not, of course,

originate in the United States, and no claim has been made in this paper that American studies in these fields were simply offshoots of American pragmatic philosophy. Nor has the claim been made that even the behavioral or actional stress in American studies of man derives solely from pragmatic sources.[5]

The present contention has simply been that American philosophical pragmatism has had a strong influence upon the behavioral orientation of psychology and the social sciences in the United States, partly in developing a climate of opinion congenial to such an orientation, and partly by providing analyses of action, sign processes, values, and evaluation which have themselves contributed both to the program and to the content of the contemporary behavioral sciences.

3.

"The Chicago School"*

This discussion of the Chicago school of pragmatism will be in two parts. First, a general consideration of the distinctive characteristics of this group of pragmatist philosophers; and secondly, some details of the late years of this group when I was a student at the University of Chicago from the fall of 1922 through the summer of 1925.

I

The phrase "the Chicago school" was applied to pragmatist thinkers at the University of Chicago by William

* This material is part of a paper given as a presidential address before the Florida Philosophical Association, November 4, 1966. There has recently appeared a much more extended account in Darnell Rucker's 1969 book *The Chicago Pragmatists*. A review-article of this book, rich in reminiscences of the period when we were fellow students at the University of Chicago, has been written by Van Meter Ames, and is to appear in *The Journal of the History of Philosophy* in July 1970.

James. In a letter of October 17, 1903, written to John Dewey, James refers to "your School (I mean your philosophic school) at the University of Chicago";[1] and "The Chicago School" is the title of James's 1904 review[2] of *Studies in Logical Theory* by Dewey and his collaborators which had appeared in 1903. Charles Peirce also used the phrase "the Chicago School" in his 1904 review of the same book in *The Nation*.[3]

Studies in Logical Theory was issued as part of the Decennial Publications of the University of Chicago. Other independent philosophical papers in the series were "Existence, Meaning and Reality in Locke's Essay and in Present Epistemology" by Addison W. Moore; "The Definition of the Psychical" by George H. Mead; "On the Genesis of the Aesthetic Categories" by James H. Tufts; and "Logical Conditions of a Scientific Treatment of Morality" by John Dewey. It was these writings that signaled the existence of "the Chicago school" and on their basis James gave it its name.

These men, Dewey, Mead, Moore, and Tufts, together with Edward Scribner Ames, constitute the Chicago school of pragmatist philosophers. In the early years philosophy and psychology were not separated, and the psychologist James Rowland Angell was an important member of the combined groups—his paper "Relation of Structural and Functional Psychology to Philosophy" also appeared in the Decennial Publications. And there were a number of other persons who collaborated in *Studies in Logical Theory* and, later, in *Creative Intelligence*. But in a distinctive sense Dewey, Mead, Moore, Tufts, and Ames were the "Chicago school," and Dewey was its acknowledged leader.

Tufts was at Chicago at its opening in 1892. He had been at the University of Michigan, a colleague of Dewey in the philosophy department. Tufts suggested to President William Rainey Harper that Dewey be brought in as head of the department, and this was done in 1894. Dewey appointed his Michigan colleague, Mead, and also Angell, who had been a student of Dewey and Mead at Michigan. Moore and Ames both took their doctorates at Chicago. Dewey remained at Chicago through 1904, when he went to Columbia University.[4]

What is characteristic of the thought of these men such that they formed a distinctive school? Light is thrown on this issue if we consider some of the early relations of Dewey with James and Peirce.*

James was enthusiastic in his review of *Studies in Logical Theory*: "It deserves the title of a new system of philosophy"; "If it be as true as it is original, its publication must be reckoned an important event. The present reviewer, for one, strongly suspects it of being true."

In the preface to the book itself the authors had agreed on "the intimate connections of logical theory with functional psychology," and had acknowledged "a pre-eminent obligation . . . to William James." Dewey, in reply to James's review, wrote to him: "None the less as far as I am concerned I have simply been rendering back in logical vocabulary what was already your own."[5]

While these words of Dewey and his co-workers are to be taken seriously, two considerations modify somewhat the picture which these acknowledgments, taken in isolation, might convey.

---

* I omit the pages on Peirce, since the relation of Peirce and Dewey has been discussed in the body of the book (1969).

Although James certainly played an important part in the movement toward a functional psychology, the bulk of his own psychology can hardly be described as functional. Present-day phenomenological psychologists, for instance, find much to their liking in James's *Principles of Psychology* and regard it as essentially a phenomenological work, superior to James's later functional and pragmatic course of thought.[6] James's distinctively functionalist paper "Does 'Consciousness' Exist?" appeared only in 1904—after *Studies in Logical Theory* and Mead's penetrating essay on "The Definition of the Psychical."

In the second place, it must not be forgotten that Dewey had been an avowed Hegelian. The focus of Hegel and his followers was upon the whole range of cultural phenomena; the orientation was to social process—however much the temporal character of social evolution was ultimately undermined by its doctrine of the Absolute. Dewey continued this process orientation as he developed from a Hegelian cultural idealist to a cultural naturalist. Dewey's own basic center of interest was ethical. Functional (and later, behavioral) psychology mainly helped him to find a new terminology to express the direction to which he in his ethical analysis was already moving. Mead maintained that James's *Psychology* was not Dewey's starting point: "Dewey passed out of his idealistic position by the way of the psychological analysis of the moral act." According to Mead, in Dewey's *Outlines of a Critical Theory of Ethics*, which was published in 1891 and makes only minor reference to James, "we find the will, the idea, and the consequences all placed inside the act, and the act itself placed only within the larger activity of the individual in society."[7] Thus contact with James at best facilitated the direction of Dewey's thought which was already under way.

Dewey's basic interest in ethics, and his early concern for applying scientific method to moral affairs, had led him into an analysis of moral action and into a consideration of the kind of inquiry appropriate to the problems encountered in such action. James's movement toward a functional psychology and Peirce's theory of inquiry fitted in with this independent direction of Dewey's thought, and served as agencies for its advancement beyond the early Hegelian framework within which Dewey began his ethical studies. Dewey's development in turn gave to the Chicago school of pragmatism a distinctive social and ethical emphasis different from the individualistic oriented pragmatism of James and the logical-analytic orientation of Peirce's pragmaticism.

II

We now turn to some characteristics of the Chicago school of pragmatism as it existed in the years 1922–1925.

Dewey had long since resigned in protest over the situation in the department of education, and had established another period of his career at Columbia University. Nevertheless, Dewey was still the major intellectual influence in the Chicago environment. He had by that time, in addition to writings already mentioned, published *Essays in Experimental Logic* (1916); *Democracy and Education* (1916); *Creative Intelligence* (1917), of which he was editor and co-author; and *Reconstruction in Philosophy* (1920).

Addison W. Moore, James H. Tufts, Edward Scribner Ames, and George H. Mead were there during the period of my study. All of them were sympathetic to Dewey's direction of thought. Dewey himself ranged over the whole field of philosophy; Moore stressed logical theory (in Dewey's sense of the term); Tufts's work was in ethics, political theory, and aesthetics; Ames concentrated on the philosophy and psychology of religion; and Mead had by that time essentially completed his philosophical version of social psychology with especial reference to the topics of mind and selfhood.

These men formed a school in a very distinctive sense: they were all elaborating aspects of a philosophic position the framework of which they held in common. Their individual work in turn fed into and influenced the further elaboration of Dewey's own comprehensive and systematic endeavors. They were not just a set of "disciples" but a group of constructive thinkers cooperatively engaged in building a philosophical edifice. I do not believe that in this sense there has been a comparable school of philosophy in the United States, and few, if indeed any, in the history of philosophy.

The Chicago pragmatists in 1922–1925 did not present the works of Dewey as texts upon which they lectured and wrote commentaries. Indeed, there was very little assignment of Dewey's writings and even very little discussion of Dewey in the classes of these men (with the exception of the classes in elementary ethics where the Dewey and Tufts *Ethics* was used as a text; and in a seminar of Moore to which reference will be made). A student in the philosophy department of those years might very well not have been conscious of it being a "school" at all. It was in the writings of Moore, Tufts, Ames, and Mead that a thoughtful student might sense that they were workers constructing a single edifice, but hardly in their classes. They were all excellent teachers and did justice to the complexity of the various subject-matters and the varieties of thought they had engendered. There was no propagandizing, though of course as good teachers their own convictions were on occasion made manifest. There was little if any talk of a general "pragmatic movement." Not only was Dewey's name used sparingly in the various courses, but there were hardly any references to James, and only once or twice a bare mention of Peirce. In none of the courses which I took was any writing of either James or Peirce assigned. I recall only one assignment of Dewey, though several papers of Dewey were reported on in seminars. Nowhere was there a trace of a doctrinaire pragmatism.

Furthermore, the staff at that time included Edwin A. Burtt and T. V. Smith. And in the visitors brought in during the summer quarter, the student encountered a variety of opinions, often quite critical of pragmatism. During my student years I worked in this way with W. K. Wright, Morris Cohen, G. Watts Cunningham, and C. I. Lewis.

The genetic and functional orientation of Dewey showed itself, however, in a number of ways. With very few exceptions the departmental courses were historical in orientation, and often the thought of the philosopher under consideration was related to his own problems in his own historical setting more fully than is usually the case in the teaching of philosophy. In the contemporary and near contemporary period the emphasis in those years was greatest upon idealist philosophers such as Francis Bradley and Bernard Bosanquet; the realist philosophers received much less attention—Bertrand Russell, for instance, was quite neglected except in an occasional seminar report. The reverse side of the historical emphasis was the comparative absence of graduate subject-matter courses such as metaphysics, philosophy of science, and symbolic logic.

I now turn to some remarks on Moore, Tufts, Ames, and Mead. I rely mainly on my class notes, upon conversations with them, and upon addresses given at the memorial services held for them.

Addison Webster Moore

Moore came closest of the Chicago group to being a "disciple" of Dewey. He had come from Cornell in 1894 expressly to study with Dewey. He was in Dewey's first seminar, and was the only member of the Chicago group to have a paper in the *Studies in Logical Theory*. James had written Dewey enthusiastically about Moore's "Existence, Meaning and Reality" paper; Dewey in reply generously said that Moore gave as much as he received. Yet Moore certainly never influenced Dewey as basically as did Mead, and he was of all the group nearest to expositor and defender of Dewey's position. This comes out in his book *Pragmatism and Its Critics*, as it did in some (but not all) of his classes.

Moore was of a sparkling mind, witty, polemical, even

at times satirical. He was frailer in constitution than his robust colleagues, and more intense. He suffered seriously from insomnia, and ill health forced him to retire several years earlier than he wished. He once told me that his health had at least cut in half what he had hoped to accomplish. Moore was at his best in two seminar sequences— Foundations of Modern Logic, and Modern Logic. The first covered the major philosophers from Descartes through Hegel; the second stressed Mill, Bradley, Bosanquet, Royce, and Dewey, with some reference to the realists Montague, Holt, Russell, and Spaulding. Moore's own position was essentially that of Dewey in *Essays in Experimental Logic*, the book which he assigned in the modern logic course when dealing with Dewey. He regarded Dewey's 1896 paper, "The Reflex Arc Concept in Psychology,"[8] as "the primary essay in the pragmatic movement." In another course he called it "the pioneer paper in the pragmatic movement." I take it that he meant that the paper was both the pioneer paper historically and the primary paper in the sense of being basic.

Moore never considered James to be the major formative influence on Dewey's thought, which he regarded as an independent development precipitated by both formal and ethical difficulties in Bradley's position ("Bradley's difficulties precipitated the pragmatic movement" is a sentence in my notes). He saw Dewey's pragmatism as essentially a revolt against absolute idealism. Instead of thought reproducing or reflecting in wholesale fashion "the real," Dewey, according to Moore, had sought the occasion for thought in a specific disturbance of the "organic circuit" comprising the organism and its environment and regarded the task of thought to be the specific resolution of such specific disturbances. In this way Dewey was said to have laid the basis for an answer to both the formal and the ethical difficulties he found in Bradley's position.

I do not wish to leave the impression that Moore was just a "defender of the faith." While Dewey's thought was back of Moore's critical analysis of other thinkers, it was never offensively on the surface. He always gave meticulous and scrupulous attention to each philosopher being considered. And as a teacher, he was superb.

James Hayden Tufts

If Moore was the logician (methodologist, epistemologist) of the post-Deweyan Chicago group, Tufts was the ethicist—or even more widely, the axiologist, since he was also concerned with aesthetics and sociopolitical theory. His two-term seminar in ethics played a role in the training of graduate students analogous to that played by Moore's seminars in logic.

Tufts had from his youth been interested in primitive societies, and had later studied a year with Sumner at Yale. He had also studied theology there with Harper, and when Harper became president of the University of Chicago he appointed Tufts to a position in philosophy. Tufts was thus at Chicago several years before Dewey. Tufts's ethical interests antedated his contacts with Dewey, but he found in Dewey the complement to his own ethical interests. He once said to me that after every half-hour conversation with Dewey he felt like writing a book. It was Tufts who suggested to Dewey the plan of the famous

Ethics, with Dewey to write the more analytic second part, and he to write the historical and much of the applied parts.

Tufts's other books continue his stress upon contemporary ethical problems: *The Ethics of Cooperation*, *The Real Business of Living*, and *America's Social Morality*. The high quality of his own theoretical ability is attested in his paper "On the Genesis of the Aesthetic Categories," and in his chapter in *Creative Intelligence* entitled "The Moral Life and the Construction of Values and Standards" (where he stressed the difference between the concepts of "good" and "ought" more strongly than any pragmatist did until C. I. Lewis).

With Tufts I had courses in aesthetics, social and political philosophy, the evolution of morality, and the seminar in ethics. All of these were historically oriented, but the first three were filled with concrete material drawn from Tufts's wide ranging in literature, anthropology, and contemporary life. I recall especially his extended treatment of romanticism and the moral development of the Hebrews. The long seminar in ethics dealt with Hobbes, Shaftesbury, Hutchinson, Butler, Clarke, Hume, Adam Smith, Bentham, Paley, Sidgwick, and T. H. Green, and with some consideration of Bosanquet, Hobhouse, and Dewey. With respect to Dewey's development away from absolute idealism, Tufts stressed the importance of Dewey's critical reaction to T. H. Green[9]—just as Moore had stressed Dewey's critical reaction to Bradley.

Perhaps because of the effect that anthropology had had upon the formation of his ethical interest, Tufts was more cautious than Dewey as to the extent to which man could or should rely on science in his moral life, though he agreed with Dewey as to the importance of introducing critical intelligence into the conduct of human affairs.

Long before Dewey had turned his attention to art, Tufts had stressed the importance of the aesthetic experience. Perhaps this was connected with his constant emphasis on the complementarity of the individual and society. He wrote in one of his books that the ideal could be expressed either as "the social individual" or as "the society which recognizes individuality." He believed that this was the ideal of American democracy, and his concrete concern was that this society progressively embody this ideal. In my class notes occur both these phrases: America is "steadily moving toward social control," and "the ultimate value is the complete person."

In *The Real Business of Living* Tufts wrote: "The finest and largest meaning of democracy is that all people should share as largely as possible in the best life." Tufts saw this as an ideal applicable to mankind. He stressed that man must pass beyond nationalism to internationalism, to a larger political organization and sense of mutual destiny. "Loyalty to mankind must finally be supreme."

Edward Scribner Ames

Ames received in 1895 the first doctorate granted by the Chicago department of philosophy. He became a member of the staff in 1900, after teaching philosophy and education at Butler College for three years. He was the last member of the Chicago school to die (in 1958 at the age of eighty-eight). Ames was my first contact with the department when I registered in 1922, and I knew him best of all its members; I saw him much during the last years of his long life.

Ames came from the Yale Divinity School to Chicago for the last year of his graduate study. He had been deeply influenced by James and by Schopenhauer, and to some extent by Comte. At Chicago he worked especially with Tufts. The effect of science upon him came through psychology and anthropology. His sense of the importance of social science was augmented by the work going on at Chicago, and especially by W. I. Thomas.

Ames was minister of the University Church of Disciples of Christ for forty years, beginning in 1900, as well as a member of the department of philosophy, in which he taught for thirty-five years. Although he gave some courses in psychology, ethics, logic, and the history of philosophy, his special domain was the psychology and philosophy of religion. His books *The Psychology of Religious Experience* and *Religion* are the major products of his thought and experience in the area of religion.

I took only one course with Ames, the psychology of religion. As I look over my notes, it seems to me to have been a model example of how problems were being handled at that time by the Chicago pragmatists in terms of their functional psychology.

The stress was upon religion as a form of social activity, and upon religious ideas as instruments to deal with difficulties encountered in that activity. Religious activity was conceived as activity to reach the highest values cherished by a social group. As the strivings for these values encountered difficulties, ceremonials arose as means to surmount these difficulties and attain the cherished goals. The ceremony is thus essentially a practical activity, and precedes the reasons given to account for it and to justify it. Myth and prayer were originally part of the ceremony. The idea of God was interpreted as the universe in its value-supportive aspects, viewed from the standpoint of a social group and idealized and personified.

Ames's activity in the Church of Disciples of Christ at the university was his attempt to enlist religion in the service of contemporary man's highest social values. His influence upon the University of Chicago community, and indeed upon the Disciples of Christ as a religious movement, was very great. The spirit of his life is vividly caught in his autobiography, edited by his son Van Meter Ames, and published under the title *Beyond Theology*.

I do not know whether Dewey had Ames explicitly in mind when he wrote his own book, *A Common Faith*, but the position he takes there is essentially the position which Ames had elaborated in his books many years earlier and which he had exemplified for forty years as pastor of his church.

George Herbert Mead

In a paper prepared for the memorial service for Mead held in 1931, Dewey said of Mead: "His mind was deeply original—in my contacts and my judgment the most original mind in philosophy in the America of the last generation. . . . I dislike to think what my own thinking might have been were it not for the seminal ideas which I derived from him."[10]

Mead had studied for a while with James, but he was

not a student of Dewey. He terminated his graduate work at Berlin to accept a position at the University of Michigan. It was then that Dewey met Mead and began the friendship which Dewey regarded as "one of the most precious possessions of my life." Dewey brought Mead to Chicago, where Mead remained until his death in 1931.

At the University of Chicago Mead taught courses in psychology as well as in philosophy. His course "Social Psychology" was the center of his teaching. It exerted year after year a strong influence upon psychologists and social scientists as well as upon students of philosophy. It was from stenographic notes of his lectures in this course (and from other student notes) that his *Mind, Self, and Society* was compiled—a book already a classic. As the title indicates, the nature of mind and selfhood was a central problem for Mead, and he accounted for their emergence in terms of language as a social process. Another basic course, "The Problem of Consciousness," attests the depth of his interest in the philosophy of mind.

Mead was more than a major social psychologist. He became increasingly interested in the place of the human mind in the cosmos. This interest—greatly stimulated by his contact with the earlier works of Whitehead—was beginning to show itself at the time I was a student, especially in a course entitled "Relativity from the Standpoint of a Pragmatist." Mead did not live to fully elaborate the cosmology toward which he was then already working, but the direction and the magnitude of his endeavor is apparent in the book based on his Carus Lectures, *The Philosophy of the Present*, and in the book formed from manuscripts left at his death, *The Philosophy of the Act*. In the light of his whole enterprise I think it is correct to say that Mead was the cosmologist of the late Chicago group, as Moore was the logician, Tufts the ethicist, and Ames the religionist.

Mead's favored mode of expression was the lecture and not the seminar. One went to Mead to listen, to experience a fine philosophic mind at work. It was as if Mead were talking aloud to the "generalized other," rather than to the assembled students. The lectures were remarkable; almost any one of them could be taken down and published as delivered. For one whole term I heard him give three lectures one right after the other in three different courses, each lecture a gem, and all this done without notes of any kind. That the lectures were carefully prepared is shown by an incident. Once when he was to give a final talk during a period officially set for the final exam (he did not give exams), he started to give the lecture meant for another course. When one of the students interrupted him to say that he must have confused the courses, Mead stood up, and with the words, "Then I have nothing to say," walked out of the room.

Mead's thoughts were like waters bubbling up from subterranean sources. Even in the form of my old lecture notes they still are fresh and sparkling. I had gone to Chicago primarily to work with Mead. The reward was indeed rich.

In concluding this account of the Chicago school of pragmatism there are two points to be added.

The first concerns the important role that the members of the Chicago group played in the liberal and progressive forces of the America of their time. Dewey's social participation was nationwide, and of a range and intensity that is fabulous. Moore, Tufts, Ames, and Mead were all deeply involved in the problems and affairs of the Chicago community—in management-labor arbitration, in the public schools, in civic matters, in settlement work. They were committed men of high moral integrity. Their philosophic orientation and their social participation were of one piece. The philosophy they built and taught was the philosophy by which they lived.

The second point concerns the termination of the Chicago school. This termination was a voluntary decision, though not made at one specific moment. There was a common feeling that the group had done its work, and that the department henceforth should manifest a diversity of viewpoints.

I was fortunate to have been a student at the University of Chicago when Moore, Tufts, Ames, and Mead were all there and with all their powers. Soon the ranks began to thin. First Moore died, then Mead, then Tufts, and then Ames. A fine theme had been sounded by Dewey, had received at Chicago an orchestral development, and had been brought in Dewey's later writings to a consummatory close.

NOTES TO APPENDIX

Pragmatism and the Behavioral Sciences

1. John Dewey, *Reconstruction in Philosophy*, 1920 ed., pp. 75–76.
2. *Ibid.*, 1948 enlarged edition, p. xxxv. See also p. xxiii.
3. *Ibid.*, 1948 enlarged edition, p. xix.
4. *The Behavioral Sciences Today*, edited by Bernard Berelson, p. 250.
5. Thus both Talcott Parsons and Florian Znaniecki regarded

sociology as the study of social action. European thinkers gave the background against which they developed their views, and their own writings make very few references to the pragmatists. Znaniecki's *Social Actions* appeared in 1936; Parsons' *The Structure of Social Action* in 1937. Mead died in 1931, but his influence was already well established in American sociology.

"The Chicago School"

1. Quoted in R. B. Perry, *The Thought and Character of William James*, vol. II, p. 524.
2. *Psychological Bulletin*, 1, 1904, 1–5.
3. Reprinted in *Collected Papers of Charles Sanders Peirce*, 8.188–90.
4. All the material in this paragraph is taken from the valuable article "John Dewey: The Chicago Years," by George Dykhuizen. I am also indebted to this article in a number of other respects. A companion article, "John Dewey in Chicago: Some Biographical Notes," is especially relevant for the circumstances which led to Dewey's resignation from the University of Chicago.
5. R. B. Perry, *op. cit.*, p. 526.
6. For example see *The Field of Consciousness* by Aron Gurvitsch, translation of his *Théorie du champs de la conscience*.
7. G. H. Mead, "The Philosophies of Royce, James, and Dewey, in their American Setting." The first quotation is from p. 228, the second from p. 227.
8. *Psychological Review*, 3, 1896, 357–70. Reprinted in Dewey's *Philosophy and Civilization* (1931) under the title "The Unit of Behavior."
9. See Dewey's article "Green's Theory of the Moral Motive," pp. 593–612.
10. Dewey's address is printed as "George Herbert Mead." The words quoted are on pp. 310–11. An article by Mead on Dewey was published after Mead's death under the title "The Philosophy of John Dewey."

Bibliography

This bibliography contains only the books and articles referred to in this book. Hence it makes no pretence of being a complete bibliography of the American pragmatic movement, nor even of its recent phase. More than four hundred books and articles on pragmatism have appeared since 1940. Very little of this material, often of high merit, has found its way into this list. The bibliographies in H. S. Thayer's *Meaning and Action* and Amelie Rorty's *Pragmatic Philosophy* are useful supplements.

For quite complete bibliographies of the major pragmatists see:

for Peirce—vol. 8 of the *Collected Papers* and vol. 2, 1966, of the *Transactions of the Charles S. Peirce Society;*

for James—John J. McDermott's *The Writings of William James* (this contains the 1920 bibliography of Ralph Barton Perry, supplemented by Ralph Barton Perry III and John J. McDermott);

for Mead—in his *Mind, Self, and Society* (also found in Andrew J. Reck's *Selected Writings of George Herbert Mead*);

for Dewey—Paul Arthur Schilpp's *The Philosophy of John Dewey* (2nd ed., 1951), and Milton H. Thomas's *John Dewey: A Centennial Bibliography.*

A surprisingly large number of the articles on pragmatism are found in the *Journal of Philosophy*, and a considerable amount of recent material appeared in *Philosophy and Phenomenological Research*, and in *The Transactions of the Charles S. Peirce Society.*

Alston, William. "Pragmatism and the Theory of Signs in Peirce," *Philosophy and Phenomenological Research* 17, 1956–57: 79–88.

Ames, Edward Scribner. *The Psychology of Religious Experience.* New York: Houghton Mifflin Co., 1910.

————. *Religion.* New York: Henry Holt and Co., 1929.

————. *Beyond Theology: The Autobiography of Edward Scribner Ames.* Edited by Van Meter Ames. Chicago: University of Chicago Press, 1959.

Ames, Van Meter. *Introduction to Beauty.* New York: Harper and Brothers, 1931.

————. "Review of Darnell Rucker's *The Chicago Pragmatists,*" *Journal of the History of Philosophy,* July 1970.

Berelson, Bernard, ed. *The Behavioral Sciences Today.* New York: Basic Books, Inc., 1963.

Bernstein, R. J., ed. *Perspectives on Peirce.* New Haven: Yale University Press, 1965.

Bikson, Tora Kay Lanto. *Peirce's Logic Treated as Semiotic.* Ph.D. dissertation, University of Missouri, 1969.

Brewster, John M. "A Behavioristic Account of the Logical Function of Universals," *Journal of Philosophy* 33, 1936: 505–14, 533–47.

Buchler, Justus. *Charles Peirce's Empiricism.* New York: Harcourt, Brace, and Co., 1939.

Burks, Arthur W. "Icon, Index, and Symbol," *Philosophy and Phenomenological Research* 9, 1948–49: 673–89.

Burtt, Edwin A. *In Search of Philosophic Understanding.* New York: New American Library, 1966.

Carnap, Rudolf. *Philosophical Foundations of Physics.* Edited by Martin Gardner. New York: Basic Books, Inc., 1966.

Dewey, John. *The Ethics of Democracy.* University of Michigan. Philosophical Papers, Second Series, no. 1. Ann Arbor, Mich.: Andrews and Co., 1888.

————. *Outlines of a Critical Theory of Ethics.* Ann Arbor, Mich.: Register Publishing Co., 1891.

————. "Green's Theory of the Moral Motive," *Philosophical Review* 1, 1892: 593–612.

————. "The Reflex Arc Concept in Psychology," *Psychological Review* 3, 1896: 357–70. Reprinted in Dewey's *Philosophy and Civilization* under the title "The Unit of Behavior."

———— et al. *Studies in Logical Theory.* Chicago: University of Chicago Press, 1903.

————and Tufts, James H. *Ethics.* New York: Henry Holt and Co., 1908.

————. "What Does Pragmatism Mean by Practical?", *Journal of Philosophy* 5, 1908: 85–99.

————. *The Influence of Darwin upon Philosophy, and Other Essays in Contemporary Thought.* New York: Henry Holt and Co., 1910.

————. *How We Think.* Boston: D. C. Heath and Co., 1910.

————. *Essays in Experimental Logic.* Chicago: University of Chicago Press, 1916.

————. "The Pragmatism of Peirce," *Journal of Philosophy* 13, 1916: 709–15.

————. *Democracy and Education.* New York: The Macmillan Co., 1916.

———— *et al. Creative Intelligence.* New York: Henry Holt and Co., 1917.

————. *Reconstruction in Philosophy.* New York: Henry Holt and Co., 1920; Boston, Mass.: The Beacon Press, 1948, enlarged edition.

————. "The Development of American Pragmatism," *Studies in the History of Ideas* 2: 353–77. New York: Columbia University Press, 1925. Reprinted in Dewey's *Philosophy and Civilization.* Originally published in French in the 1922 *Revue de Métaphysique et de Morale.*

————. *Experience and Nature.* Chicago: Open Court Publishing Co., 1925 and 1929.

————. *The Public and Its Problems.* New York: Henry Holt and Co., 1927.

————. *The Quest for Certainty.* New York: Minton, Balch and Co., 1929.

————. *Individualism, Old and New.* New York: Minton, Balch and Co., 1930.

————. "George Herbert Mead," *Journal of Philosophy* 28, 1931: 309–14.

————. *Philosophy and Civilization.* New York: Minton, Balch and Co., 1931.

————. *Art as Experience.* New York: Minton, Balch and Co., 1934.

————. *A Common Faith.* New Haven: Yale University Press, 1934.

————. "Peirce's Theory of Quality," *Journal of Philosophy* 32, 1935: 701–08.

————. *Liberalism and Social Action.* New York: G. P. Putnam's Sons, 1935.

————. *Logic: The Theory of Inquiry.* New York: Henry Holt and Co., 1938.

————. *Experience and Education.* New York: The Macmillan Co., 1938.

————. *Theory of Valuation,* vol. 2, no. 4, of the *International Encyclopedia of Unified Science.* Chicago: University of Chicago Press, 1939.

————. *Freedom and Culture.* New York: G. P. Putnam's Sons, 1939.

————. "The Objectivism-Subjectivism of Modern Philosophy," *Journal of Philosophy* 38, 1941: 533–42. (Reprinted in *Problems of Men.*)

————. *Problems of Men.* New York: Philosophical Library, 1946.

————. "The Field of 'Value'" in *Value: A Cooperative Inquiry.* Edited by Ray Lepley. New York: Columbia University Press, 1949.

————. "Experience, Knowledge, and Value" in *The Philosophy of John Dewey.* Edited by Paul A. Schilpp, 2nd ed. New York: Tudor Publishing Co., 1951, 517–608.

Dykhuizen, George. "John Dewey: The Chicago Years," *Journal of the History of Philosophy* 2, 1964: 227–53.

————. "John Dewey in Chicago: Some Biographical Notes," *Journal of the History of Philosophy* 3, 1965: 217–33.

Fisch, Max H. "Alexander Bain and the Genealogy of Pragmatism," *Journal of the History of Ideas* 15, 1954: 413–44.

Fitzgerald, John J. *Peirce's Theory of Signs as Foundation for Pragmatism.* The Hague: Mouton and Co., 1966.

Gallie, W. D. *Peirce and Pragmatism.* London: Penguin Books, 1952.

Gurvitsch, Aron. *The Field of Consciousness.* Pittsburgh: Duquesne University Press, 1964.

Hartshorne, Charles. "Charles Peirce's 'One Contribution to Philosophy' and His Most Serious Mistake," in *Studies in the Philosophy of Charles Sanders Peirce: Second Series.* Edited by Edward C. Moore and Richard S. Robin. Amherst: University of Massachusetts Press, 1964.

Hocutt, Max O. "The Logical Foundations of Peirce's Aesthetics," *Journal of Aesthetics and Art Criticism* 21, 1962: 157–66.

Holmes, Larry. "Peirce on Self-Control," *Transactions of the Charles S. Peirce Society* 2, 1966: 113–30.

Hook, Sidney, ed. *John Dewey: Philosopher of Science and Freedom.* New York: Dial Press, 1950.

———. *Quest for Being.* New York: St. Martin's Press, 1961.

James, William. *The Principles of Psychology.* New York: Henry Holt and Co., 1890.

———. "The Moral Philosopher and the Moral Life," *International Journal of Ethics* 1, 1891: 330–54.

———. *The Varieties of Religious Experience.* New York: Longmans, Green and Co., 1902.

———. "Does 'Consciousness' Exist?" *Journal of Philosophy* 1, 1904: 477–91. Reprinted in *Essays in Radical Empiricism.*

———. "The Chicago School," *Psychological Bulletin* 1, 1904: 1–5.

———. *Pragmatism.* New York: Longmans, Green and Co., 1907.

———. *The Meaning of Truth: A Sequel to "Pragmatism."* New York: Longmans, Green and Co., 1909.

———. *A Pluralistic Universe.* New York: Longmans, Green and Co., 1909.

———. *Some Problems of Philosophy.* New York: Longmans, Green and Co., 1911.

———. *Essays in Radical Empiricism.* Edited by Ralph Barton Perry. New York: Longmans, Green and Co., 1912.

Kallen, Horace M. *Art and Freedom.* New York: Duell, Sloan and Pearce, 1942.

———. *The Liberal Spirit.* Ithaca, N.Y.: Cornell University Press, 1948.

———. *Secularism Is the Will of God.* New York: Twayne Publishers, 1954.

———. *Cultural Pluralism and the American Idea.* Philadelphia: University of Pennsylvania Press, 1956.

Keen, Tom Clifton. "George Herbert Mead's Social Theory of Meaning and Experience." Ph.D. dissertation, Ohio State University, 1968.

Kennedy, Gail, ed. *Pragmatism and American Culture.* Boston: D. C. Heath and Co., 1950.

Kurtz, Paul, ed. *Sidney Hook and the Contemporary World.* New York: John Day, 1968.

Lenzen, Victor F. "Charles S. Peirce as Astronomer," in *Studies in the Philosophy of Charles Sanders Peirce, Second Series*. Edited by Edward C. Moore and Richard S. Robin. Amherst: University of Massachusetts Press, 1964.
————. "The Contributions of Charles S. Peirce to Metrology," *Proceedings of the American Philosophical Society* 109, 1965: 29–46.
Lepley, Ray, ed. *Value: A Cooperative Inquiry*. New York: Columbia University Press, 1949.
Lewis, Clarence Irving. "A Pragmatic Conception of the *A Priori*," *Journal of Philosophy* 20, 1923: 169–77.
————. *Mind and the World-Order*. New York: Charles Scribner's Sons, 1929.
————. "Meaning and Action," *Journal of Philosophy* 36, 1939: 572–76.
————. "Some Logical Considerations Concerning the Mental," *Journal of Philosophy* 38, 1941: 225–33.
————. *An Analysis of Knowledge and Valuation*. LaSalle, Ill.: Open Court Publishing Co., 1946.
————. *The Ground and Nature of the Right*. New York: Columbia University Press, 1955.
————. *The Philosophy of C. I. Lewis*. Edited by Paul Arthur Schilpp. LaSalle, Ill.: The Open Court Publishing Co., 1968.
————. *Values and Imperatives*. Edited by John F. Lange. Stanford, Calif.: Stanford University Press, 1969.
McDermott, John J., ed. *The Writings of William James*. New York: Modern Library, 1968.
Mead, George Herbert. "The Relations of Psychology and Philology," *Psychological Bulletin* 1, 1904: 375–91.
————. "The Imagination in Wundt's Treatment of Myth and Religion," *Psychological Bulletin* 3, 1906: 393–99.
————. "A Behavioristic Account of the Significant Symbol," *Journal of Philosophy* 19, 1922: 157–63.
————. "Scientific Method and the Moral Sciences," *International Journal of Ethics* 33, 1923: 229–47. Also included in *Selected Writings of George Herbert Mead*. Edited by Andrew J. Reck.
————. "The Genesis of the Self and Social Control," *International Journal of Ethics* 35, 1924–1925: 251–77. Also included in *Selected Writings of George Herbert Mead*. Edited by Andrew J. Reck.
————. "The Nature of Aesthetic Experience," *International Journal of Ethics* 36, 1926: 382–92. Reprinted with some omissions in his *The Philosophy of the Act*, 454–57.
————. "The Objective Reality of Perspectives," *Proceedings of the Sixth International Congress of Philosophy* 1926, published in 1927. Also included in *The Philosophy of the Present*, and in *Selected Writings of George Herbert Mead*. Edited by Andrew J. Reck.
————. "A Pragmatic Theory of Truth," in *Studies in the Nature of Truth*, University of California Publications in Philosophy 11, 1929: 65–88. Also included in *The Selected Writings of George Herbert Mead*. Edited by Andrew J. Reck.

————. "The Philosophies of Royce, James, and Dewey, in their American Setting," *International Journal of Ethics* 40, 1930: 211–31. Also included in *The Selected Writings of George Herbert Mead*. Edited by Andrew J. Reck.

————. *The Philosophy of the Present*. Edited by Arthur E. Murphy. Chicago: Open Court Publishing Co., 1932.

————. *Mind, Self, and Society*. Edited by Charles Morris. Chicago: University of Chicago Press, 1934.

————. "The Philosophy of John Dewey," *International Journal of Ethics* 46, 1935: 64–81.

————. *The Philosophy of the Act*. Edited by Charles Morris with the collaboration of John M. Brewster, Albert M. Dunham, and David L. Miller. Chicago: University of Chicago Press, 1938.

Miller, David L. *Individualism: Personal Achievement and the Open Society*. Austin, Texas: University of Texas Press, 1967.

Mills, C. Wright. *Sociology and Pragmatism*. New York: Paine-Whitman Publishers, 1964.

Moore, Addison W. *Pragmatism and Its Critics*. Chicago: University of Chicago Press, 1910.

Moore, Edward C. and Robin, Richard S., eds. *Studies in the Philosophy of Charles Sanders Peirce, Second Series*. Amherst: University of Massachusetts Press, 1964.

Moore, Edward C. *American Pragmatism: Peirce, James, and Dewey*. New York: Columbia University Press, 1961.

Morris, Charles. *Six Theories of Mind*. Chicago: University of Chicago Press, 1932.

————. "Pragmatism and Metaphysics," *The Philosophical Review* 43, 1934: 549–64.

————. "Peirce, Mead, and Pragmatism," *Philosophical Review* 47, 1938: 109–27.

————. *Paths of Life: Preface to a World Religion*. New York: Harper and Brothers, 1942.

————. "Axiology as the Science of Preferential Behavior," in *Value: A Cooperative Inquiry*. Edited by Ray Lepley. New York: Columbia University Press, 1949.

————. *Signs, Language, and Behavior*. New York: Prentice-Hall, 1946; George Braziller, 1955.

————. *Varieties of Human Value*. Chicago: University of Chicago Press, 1956.

————. *Signification and Significance: A Study of the Relations of Signs and Values*. Cambridge: Massachusetts Institute of Technology Press, 1964.

Murphey, Murray G. *The Development of Peirce's Philosophy*. Cambridge, Mass.: Harvard University Press, 1961.

————. "Kant's Children: The Cambridge Pragmatists," *Transactions of the Charles S. Peirce Society* 4, 1968: 3–33.

Murphy, Arthur E. "Objective Relativism in Dewey and Whitehead," *Philosophical Review* 36, 1927: 121–44.

————. "Concerning Mead's *The Philosophy of the Act*," *Journal of Philosophy* 36, 1939: 85–103.

———. "Dewey's Epistemology and Metaphysics," in *The Philosophy of John Dewey*. Edited by Paul Arthur Schilpp, 2nd ed. New York: Tudor Publishing Co., 1951, 195–225.

———. *Reason and the Common Good*. Englewood Cliffs, N.J.: Prentice-Hall, Inc., 1963.

Nagel, Ernest. "Charles Peirce's Guess at the Riddle," *Journal of Philosophy* 30, 1933: 365–86.

———. *Sovereign Reason*. Glencoe, Ill.: The Free Press, 1954.

———. *The Structure of Science*. New York: Harcourt, Brace and World, 1961.

Parsons, Talcott. *The Structure of Social Action*, 2nd ed. New York: The Free Press, 1958.

Peirce, Charles Sanders. *The Collected Papers of Charles Sanders Peirce*. Cambridge: Harvard University Press, 1931–58. Volumes 1–6 edited by Charles Hartshorne and Paul Weiss; volumes 7 and 8 edited by Arthur W. Burks.

1	*Principles of Philosophy*	1931
2	*Elements of Logic*	1932
3	*Exact Logic*	1933
4	*The Simplest Mathematics*	1933
5	*Pragmatism and Pragmaticism*	1934
6	*Scientific Metaphysics*	1935
7	*Science and Philosophy*	1958
8	*Reviews, Correspondence, and Bibliography*	1958

Perry, Ralph Barton. *General Theory of Value*. New York: Longmans, Green and Co., 1926.

———. *The Thought and Character of William James*. Boston: Little, Brown and Co., 1935.

———. *Realms of Value*. Cambridge, Mass.: Harvard University Press, 1954.

Potter, Vincent G. *Charles S. Peirce: On Norms and Ideals*. Amherst: University of Massachusetts Press, 1967.

Quine, Willard Van Orman. *Word and Object*. Cambridge: M.I.T. Press. New York: John Wiley and Sons, 1960.

Rao, K. Ramakrishna. *Gandhi and Pragmatism*. Calcutta: Oxford and IBH Publishing Co., 1968.

Reck, Andrew J., ed. *Selected Writings of George Herbert Mead*. Indianapolis, Ind.: The Bobbs-Merrill Co., 1964.

——— ed. *Introduction to William James*. Bloomington, Ind.: Indiana University Press, 1967.

———. *The New American Philosophers*. Baton Rouge: Louisiana State University Press, 1968.

Rorty, Amelie, ed. *Pragmatic Philosophy*. Garden City, New York: Doubleday and Company, 1966.

Rucker, Darnell. *The Chicago Pragmatists*. Minneapolis: University of Minnesota Press, 1969.

Schilpp, Paul Arthur, ed. *The Philosophy of John Dewey*, 2nd ed. New York: Tudor Publishing Co., 1951.

——— ed. *The Philosophy of C. I. Lewis*. LaSalle, Ill.: The Open Court Publishing Co., 1968.

Schneider, Herbert W. *A History of American Philosophy.* New York: Columbia University Press, 1946; 2nd ed., 1963.

Thayer, H. S. *The Logic of Pragmatism.* New York: Humanities Press, 1952.

———. *Meaning and Action: A Critical History of Pragmatism.* Indianapolis, Ind.: The Bobbs-Merrill Co., 1968.

Thomas, Milton Halsey. *John Dewey: A Centennial Bibliography.* Chicago: University of Chicago Press, 1962.

Thompson, Manley. *The Pragmatic Philosophy of C. S. Peirce.* Chicago: University of Chicago Press, 1953.

Tufts, James Hayden. "On the Genesis of the Aesthetic Categories," *Decennial Publications of the University of Chicago, First Series, III, Part 2.* Chicago: University of Chicago Press, 1903.

———. *The Real Business of Living.* New York: Henry Holt and Co., 1918.

———. *The Ethics of Cooperation.* Boston: Houghton Mifflin, 1918.

———. *America's Social Morality.* New York: Henry Holt and Co., 1933.

Wells, Rulon. "Peirce as an American," in *Perspectives on Peirce.* Edited by R. J. Bernstein. New Haven: Yale University Press, 1965.

White, Morton G. *Toward Reunion in Philosophy.* Cambridge, Mass.: Harvard University Press, 1956.

———. *Social Thought in America.* New York: Viking Press, 1949; enlarged edition, Boston: Beacon Press, 1957.

Whitehead, Alfred North. "John Dewey and His Influence," in *The Philosophy of John Dewey.* Edited by Paul Arthur Schilpp, 2nd ed., 477–78. New York: Tudor Publishing Co., 1951.

Wiener, Philip P. *Evolution and the Founders of Pragmatism.* Cambridge, Mass.: Harvard University Press, 1949.

Wild, John. *The Radical Empiricism of William James.* New York: Doubleday and Co., 1969.

Znaniecki, Florian. *Social Actions.* New York: Russell and Russell, 1936.

Addendum:

Ames, Edward Scribner. *Prayers and Meditations.* Edited by Van Meter Ames. Chicago, The Disciples Divinity House, 1970.

INDEX

on "conversation of ges-
tures," 34

cosmology of, 128–136; 140,
n.33

conception of an object, 71–
74

current work on, 145–146

on Dewey, 152

ethics of, 108, n.20; 150–
151

and evolutionary biology,
7–8

influence on behavioral
science, 170–172

influence on Dewey, 37

"principle of sociality" of,
128–132

theory of meaning of, 35–36

theory of mind of, 126–127,
131; 138, n.21

theory of the self, 127–128

on language, 33–36, 126–
128

on the nature of ideas, 36

on philosophy of history, 78–
79

on the problematic situation,
78, n.8

on religion, 101–104

on taking the role of the
other, 72

on "vocal gestures," 35

and Watsonian behaviorism,
43, n.2

Mead, Henry C. A., 45, n.19

Meaning,
and the gesture, 34–36

pragmatic view of, 1–3; 42,
n.1

Metaphysical rationalism, 67–
68

Merleau-Ponty, Maurice, 153,
n.11

Merton, Robert K., 172

Metaphysics, Peirce on, 110–
111

Methodology, overview of pragmatic theory of, 75–77

Mill, John Stuart, 7

Miller, David L., 146; 153,
n.2

Mills, C. Wright, 154, n.13

Mind,
Dewey's theory of, 163
Mead's theory of, 126–128;
138, n.21

Moore, Addison W., 175, 179,
181–183

Moore, Edward C., 79, n.20

Morality and democracy, 94–
96

Morris, Charles, 45, n.23; 46,
n.26; 47, n.39; 80, n.30;
108, n.10, n.12; 109,
n.29, n.31; 136, n.2; 138,
n.20; 138, n.22; 153, n.1

Murphy, Arthur E., 79, n.27;
80, n.35; 134; 138, n.30

Murphey, Murray G., 44, n.9;
78, n.6; 147

Nagel, Ernest, 43, n.3; 78, n.9;
80, n.36; 138, n.30